KU-674-204

GOD AND MAN

Church of England Chaplaincy
to the
University of Bristol

GOD AND MAN

METROPOLITAN
ANTHONY OF SOUROZH

HODDER AND STOUGHTON
LONDON SYDNEY AUCKLAND TORONTO

Copyright © *1971* and *1974* by Metropolitan Anthony. First printed *1971*. This edition *1974*. ISBN *o 340 18230 X*. All rights reserved. No part of this publication may be reproduced or transmitted in any form or by any means, electronic or mechanical, including photocopy, recording, or any information storage and retrieval system, without permission in writing from the publisher. This book is sold subject to the condition that it shall not, by way of trade or otherwise, be lent, re-sold, hired out or otherwise circulated without the publisher's prior consent in any form of binding other than that in which this is published and without a similar condition including this condition being imposed on the subsequent purchaser. Printed in Great Britain for Hodder and Stoughton Limited, St. Paul's House, Warwick Lane, London EC4P 4AH by Hazell Watson and Viney Limited, Aylesbury, Bucks.

CONTENTS

CHAPTER ONE

ATHEIST AND CHRISTIAN—
A DIALOGUE[1]

Marghanita Laski and Metropolitan Anthony of Sourozh

I

Miss Laski: You believe in God, and you think this is good and right. I don't believe in God, and I think it's good and right. Now we're neither of us frivolous people, we're serious, we've reached our decision as carefully as we can. There's a lot of people like me, there's a lot of people, probably a lot more people, like you. How do you explain this basic, one could say, this *fundamental* difference?

Metropolitan Anthony: I really don't know how to explain it but it seems to me that the word 'belief' is misleading. It gives an impression of something optional, which is within our powers to choose or not. What I feel very strongly about it, is that I believe because I know that God exists, and I'm puzzled how you manage not to know.

M. L.: This brings me to the next thing I wanted to ask you, which is about faith. I know that faith is a major Christian virtue but to me it's nearer a vice and I cannot

[1] Transcript of televised interviews, transmitted 5th and 12th July, 1970; with grateful acknowledgement to the BBC.

see why you need it. When you say 'I know that God exists' and many people do say this for one reason or another because they've experienced God or because they see God in the shape of the universe. But if you know, you don't need faith. And if you don't know, to me as an unbeliever, it's almost throwing away the most important thing about a human being, to substitute faith for not knowing. To me, the right thing when you don't know is to wait on knowledge or to say 'I don't know'. If you know that God exists, why should faith be considered a virtue?

M.A.: I think it's a question of the definition of faith. I remember having read in a rather facetious theological book a definition of faith as the ability which grown-ups possess to assert that things are true when they know that they are not true.

M.L.: That's rather nice ...

M.A.: If that is faith, I'm afraid I don't possess it. I think faith is best defined in the words of the Epistle to the Hebrews, when the writer says 'Faith is certainty about things invisible.' It is certainty, that is the operative word, and things which are invisible are not simply things imagined. Speaking for instance of myself and a number of other people, I'm sure we began with an experience that was totally convincing. Now at a certain moment this experience faded away, as does every experience of beauty, of love, of joy, of pain. There is a moment when it is no longer actual, but the certainty of it has remained. And this is the moment when faith comes into it. But faith doesn't mean credulity; it means that the certainty remains about something which is not our actual present experience of things.

M. L.: If you use the word faith, surely it must imply that you have faith in the face of possible doubt? But if you have certainty, then there's no room for doubt, and so I'm sorry, I can't see any need for faith—isn't certainty enough?

M. A.: You are in the same position as I in a way. You have a certainty, concerning the non-existence of God, which in a way is an act of faith, because you have as little evidence you can produce outwardly as I have to produce outwardly.

M. L.: Wouldn't you say there was a fundamental difference in the way of thinking about, or of approaching problems of the invisible, that there could be a temperamental preference for having certainty about the invisible, and for reserving judgement about the invisible?

M. A.: I'm not sure, I think my attitude to things is very much determined by the kind of education I have had. I was trained to be a scientist and I treat things as experimental science—perhaps wrongly, perhaps rightly. But as far as faith is concerned, for instance, I started with something which was an experience which seemed to be convincing, that God does exist. Doubt comes into it not as questioning this fundamental experience but as questioning my intellectual workings out of it. And in that respect the doubt of the believer should be as creative, as daring, as joyful, almost as systematic as the doubt of a scientist who, having discovered facts that have convinced him up to a point of something, will begin to find the flaw in his reasoning, the error in his system, or new facts that will invalidate his model of the universe.

M. L.: But his moment of discovering, as it seems to him, a new pattern in the universe, is equally convincing whether his examination of the pattern shows it to be true or false. The scientist will no doubt value the feeling that comes with the new discovery, but he wouldn't regard that feeling as validating, as you say; he would afterwards make tests and so on. But you don't, do you, admit an experience of feeling as if God exists which doesn't necessarily say whether God exists or not?

M. A.: I don't think it's wholly a question of feeling. I don't think for instance that feeling can be simply unreasonable or completely absurd, and yet kept against every other evidence. But I would say for instance if you transfer, for a moment, from faith in God to other fields —music, say—from the point of view of a scientist, music can be put in drawing, in line, in mathematical formulae. When you've got them all it does not give you a clue as to whether this is a beautiful piece of music or whether it is just discordant noise. There is a moment when you listen and you say this is music and not simply noise.

M. L.: Certainly, although one of the things I most want to know about is why good music, good poetry, good art, has the effect on us it does, and I always assume that experiences of God include such a patterning. I as an atheist would never want to doubt the profound knowledge that the churches, synagogues, mosques, have acquired over the centuries, into human nature, into human thought, into human physical responses. Now you've written greatly about interior prayer and even before I read your book I was very much interested in this because it seemed to me clearly that it worked. That is to say, people who attempted contemplative prayer received benefit from it. And this I have tried, I have tried it a great deal recently, because I've just had a very bad slipped disc, and I don't like painkillers. And it seemed to me that to try contemplative prayer, as St Gregory describes it, meditating on the Lord's Prayer for instance, might help my pain. And indeed it did. So I assume that here the Church has discovered a mental technique which is therapeutic, which is beneficial. But it seems to me that in the case of this experience of prayer, as in other experiences called religious, the Church has, so to speak, pre-empted them, said 'These are our experiences, these lead to God.' I'm not pretending my attempts compare with anything that a trained religious could do, but are you not holding to yourselves and giving explanations which are unacceptable to atheists of various techniques and modes of living that could help all humanity, perhaps even in this time of recourse to drugs—could help humanity with greater need than ever before?

M. A.: As far as techniques and methods are concerned, I quite agree that you are right, and I could give you an example in your favour as it were, about a group of drug addicts who by chance read *The Cloud of Unknowing* and addressed themselves to a priest, not to me, to say: 'We have discovered that this is exactly what we are looking for and it would be a much cheaper thing for us to get it that way than through the drugs we are using—'

M. L.: And much healthier.

M. A.: Much healthier. And we have experience now of a number of drug addicts for instance who discover through meditation what they were looking for through drugs, and move away from drugs into another world. As far as technique is concerned I think it is completely true, because techniques are founded on our common humanity. Whatever the object you pursue, your thinking is your human thinking, your emotions and feelings are your human emotions and so forth. What the believer would say is that for some reason, the same kind of reason that makes you recognise beauty in music, in nature, in art and so on, he would say: 'This experience which I had is neither my emotions nor my wishful thinking, nor my physical condition at that moment; it was a meeting with something different, profoundly other than myself, and which I cannot trace back even with decent knowledge of sociology, or psychology, or biology, to anything which is me, and within me.'

M.L.: This is the fundamental difference between us, isn't it? Whether this feeling that we have encountered is something other than oneself, is a self-induced feeling or is an other-induced feeling, an over-derived feeling. Is this not what separates us most?

M.A.: Yes. A believer would say: 'I objectively know that He exists, which means I have knowledge acquired and not manufactured.' But doesn't it apply in the same way to things like irrational experiences in common life? Like love, like the sense of beauty, in art, music and so on?

M.L.: I would guess that the sense of beauty is irrational only for the present until explained. I always think of the philosopher Hume, who two hundred years ago said we know that bread does us good but we shall never know why and of course now we do know why. And I think we shall, perhaps in the not very distant future, come to learn what kind of patterning it is that affects us and that we call beautiful.

M. A.: That may well be, but why don't you think that we may by the same process come to a point when by the study, say, of brainwaves and that kind of thing, we will be able to discover that at such a moment something has intruded or come into our experience which is not intrinsic to our physical body. Logically, it's as credible as the other one.

M. L.: This is what I would most like to know and of course if the experiment worked your way, there would be no alternative to being a believer. I simply suspect it would work my way. But supposing I had, as any of us unbelievers might have, a sudden experience of the kind you describe as certainty that God existed. Supposing that it didn't take place in any religious context. Let's say like St Ignatius Loyola, I was sitting by a river. Now I know I was brought up a Jew, but I've lived in England, which is as they say the country of a hundred religions and one sauce, why should anything follow from this? I can understand that it would be sensible to join a religion for fear of the kind of arrogant madness that falls upon people who think that they have a direct personal line to God, but from this experience of God, what should lead me to suppose I've encountered a Christian, a Jewish, a Moslem God? That he would want me to be a Methodist or a Russian Orthodox or Church of England? What should make one take a step further than having this experience and saying: 'Fine, I now have the certainty that God exists'?

M. A.: It would proceed in different steps—if you had, and I'm certain one can have an experience of God outside any context of previous religiosity or religious background, then you will probably discover that if God does exist it has immediate implications as to your situation with regard to men in general . . .

M. L.: Please explain because this is what I want to understand.

M. A.: Readily. My experience in childhood was that life was violent, brutal, heartless, that men were to one another adversaries and causes of suffering, that there were on the whole just a few, the closest around you, who belonged together, and who were no danger to you. And my situation when I was a young teenager, was that all these people were dangers. One had to fight, to overcome in order to survive, and eventually to hit back as hard as one could in order to win the day.

M. L.: This was truly your situation, I believe, wasn't it?

M. A.: That was the experience I had, in a slum school, and in the early years of revolution and so on—not in Russia but abroad. Now, when I discovered God and I discovered Him in connection with the Gospel, the first thing that struck me is that here was a God for whom everyone was meaningful, who was not segregating people, who was not the God of the good versus the bad, the God of the believer versus the unbeliever, the God of one type versus another. That everyone existed for Him as a completely meaningful and valuable person. And if I had discovered that God, then that was the attitude I had to discover with regard to all my surroundings. And you know, I felt with amazement that the fact that I had discovered that God was such, and that that was His relatedness to everyone else, upturned me completely. I looked around and I no longer saw the detestable hateful creatures, but people who were in relationship with Him, and with whom I could come into a new relationship, if I believed about them what God believes about them.

M. L.: But it is a fact that non-believers can have this experience of respectful love, charitable love, to all creatures, without the need for God. I'm not a good Socialist, but I think that people who are really good Socialists, in the basic sense, not the political sense of the word, have this feeling. It's not necessary to have God to have the sense of the worth of each human being.

M. A.: No, I don't mean to say that it is necessary. I would say it is not necessary to know that God exists to be a human being, and not below the mark as I was quite definitely. Neither is it necessary I would say, to know that God exists for Him to exist in fact. To me the problem of God is this. He is not something I need to have a world outlook. I don't need God to fill gaps in my world outlook. I have discovered that He exists and I can't help it, exactly in the same way as I have discovered facts in science. He is a fact for me, and that's why He has significance and plays a role in a way exactly in the same sense in which having discovered that a person exists, life becomes different from the moment before you had become aware of the person.

M. L.: Could I ask you to be a bit concrete about this? For instance this is rather a debating point I'm going to make, but I think it's a valid one. For the past five hundred years, since science escaped from the bounds of the Church, it's leapt ahead, so that it's a commonplace now to say that our technological, our scientific, knowledge is beyond our moral capacity. The Church, on the other hand, has had two thousand years to develop our moral capacity, if this is one of its functions. But you have said that one can come to this awareness of the real individual —what's the Christian word I want?—for the existence, the respectful existence of every human being. And this entails, I think, a kind of behaviour to human beings which makes a link between belief in God and morals. Is there a necessary link between belief in God and morals? What is it? And since the Church doesn't seem in two thousand years to have made us good—in fact I would claim that it's secular thought that has done most to improve us over the past two hundred years—can the Church be said to have fulfilled this function? In other words, how do morals follow from belief in God? Why has the Church failed to make us moral beings?

M. A.: I think quite certainly morals should follow our belief in God because if we see the world structured around a certain number of great principles, it should make a difference to our behaviour . . .

M. L.: What are the great principles?

M. A.: Love, let us say . . . love, justice.

M. L.: Because you feel love when you encounter God? Because God seems to be a creature of love and justice?— I mean where do these virtues come into the encounter with God?

M. A.: Let me limit myself to the Gospel which will be easier than to try to embrace a wider field. The whole teaching of the Gospel is really a teaching about loving. Now the fact that we fall short of it condemns us, doesn't make the declaration of it less true. I'm quite prepared to say that individually and collectively we have fallen very short of that ideal. Now what I'm more doubtful about, is what you said about secular thought because my impression is that west European secular thought at least, or the secular thought developed from west European culture, is so impregnated with the Gospel. For instance the notion of the value of the person, is something which the Gospel has introduced into ancient society which simply didn't possess it. And there are so many things which now have become common ground, universally accepted, which were novelties in their time and which now work in society as leaven works in dough.

M. L.: I would agree with you completely about this. I'm only saying that over the past two hundred years, at least since the middle of the eighteenth century, these principles which do seem to me to be the glory of western civilisation, have passed effectively into the hands of the seculars and from the hands of the religious, that insofar as there has been a moral leap forward over this period, and I think there has been one, it's not I think, the churches, the synagogues, that we have to thank for it.

M. A.: There are two things that strike me—the one is that the believers have had and still have a most unfortunate tendency to escape the difficulties and the problems of life into 'worship' in inverted commas.

M. L.: Yes, I'm glad you brought that up.

M. A.: That quite certainly. It's much easier to retire to one's room and say: 'Oh God, give bread to the hungry,' than to do something about it. I have just been in America and someone was making discourse about his readiness to give his life for the hungry and the needy, and I asked him why he was a chain smoker and didn't give simply a packet of cigarettes for it.

M. L.: And I can throw another example at you. All of us who have children and meet a lot of young people . . . meet the people who ask for more love in the world but find it impossible to give it to the older generation.

M. A.: Yes, that's true too. So that is quite definite. We have been escaping into a world of irresponsible prayer, instead of realising that if I say to God, 'Here is a need. Help,' I must be prepared to hear God answer within me, without waiting for a revelation, 'You have seen that —well go and do it.' So that is a way in which we have failed, and which is one of the reasons why we have gone wrong.

M. L.: Could I suggest that another reason why I think you and the secular do-gooders also have failed is because of a rejection of the world, not just as you say, going into one's room and failing to do the good that lies to hand, but a feeling that the world and particularly the urban world of today, is a hell—a Satanic mill, a place to be avoided. There's no gaiety in religion, for instance, there's no enjoyment of a jolly life. The pleasures that we normally take in society, even if you like, the pleasures of amassing possessions, of sitting in our little castles with our refrigerators round us and our children playing at our feet—these to me are healthful pleasures. But I think that serious people, serious religious people, serious non-religious people, have always regarded these things that we genuinely enjoy as human animals, as clogs in the way of the good life.

M. A.: I think they are right up to a point. I think it takes a great deal of mastery of self not to forget what is deepest in oneself to the profit of what is more superficial. It's easier to be superficial than deep, it's easier to be on that level rather than face things that may be tragic. You see the difficulty is that we have made it into a false moral attitude, into an attitude that if you are a Christian you must be stern, almost sinister, never laugh—

M. L.: Or very, very simple, so simple and innocent that the realities of life seem irrelevant to you.

M. A.: Yes. But if you are really aware of things, of how tragic life is, then there is restraint in your enjoyment. Joy is another thing. One can possess a great sense of inner joy and elation, but enjoying the outer aspects of life with the awareness of so many people suffering and so on, is something which I find difficult. When I was a professional man, we made a decision with my mother never to live beyond the minimum which we needed for shelter and food because we thought and I still think, that whatever you spend above that, is stolen from someone else who needs it while you don't. That doesn't make you sinister, it gives you a sense of joy in sharing, and in giving and receiving. But I do feel that as long as there is one person who is hungry, excess of happiness—excess of amenities—is theft . . .

M. L.: And yet each one person is so vulnerable, so prone to tragedy, so likely to fall into danger that when I see people, for instance on a beach, with excessive possessions and enjoying themselves excessively, here I think, is gaiety, a little happiness stored, a moment of gaiety that is not wrong.

M. A.: I wouldn't say it is wrong. I think it could be deeper and it could be more permanent. One of the problems of the modern person is that we have so much that we no longer enjoy little things. Say, in the years when life was extremely hard, in my experience, the slightest joy was a miracle. Now, my level of miracle has come up; it takes more for me to find that things are so miraculous.

M. L.: Yes, and yet sometimes people rediscover simplicity through excess. I'm not morally disagreeing with what you are saying but I am wondering whether this—to put forward such a moral point as you do—isn't to impose guilt on most of us who are not so austere. This would be a general charge, not against you only.

M. A.: Guilt is always wrong and guilt is a sickly attitude to life. It's useless. It's destructive and it does away with the very sense that all things are possible, that one can put things right. No, I believe that guilt is wrong but I think that it is a challenge of greater joy. If I say, for instance, I won't do this because I can have the joy of sharing, instead of parasitically, in a predatory way, devouring it for myself, I'm not diminishing my joy and I'm not developing a sense of guilt.

M. L.: The only thing I'd say is that if you are wrong—guilty—have done wrong, it's better to bear it yourself than to put it on to other people. It may be necessary to bear your own guilt and work through it.

M. A.: I think it's better to leave the word guilt alone and *do* something . . .

M. L.: Certainly, do something, but don't push it on to somebody else.

M. A.: I don't see any advantage in pushing it on somebody else except if somebody is prepared, in terms of affection, friendship, love or whatever you call it, I mean relatedness to you, to share with you your problem, your predicament, not your sense of guilt, not your drowning, but your getting out of it.

M. L.: I've been pushing my questions at you and you've been very generous, but have I left out—I'm sure I have —some important area that you would like to put forward? Have I given you insufficient scope to say what's really important to you?

M. A.: No, I think it was very exciting as it was. We never can cover all the ground, anyhow. What I feel, to put it in two very short statements about God and religion, is that to me God is not someone I need to fill gaps. It's someone I have got to accept because from the experience of life I have He does exist; I can't avoid the fact. And the second thing is that all the morals that develop from His existence are part not of a duty to Him or a duty to people— I don't like the word duty—but an act of happiness and gratitude for God and for people, and that links with worship—a worshipful attitude to God, a worshipful attitude to people, a worshipful attitude to life; I think the sense of worship and joy and of a challenge which will make me grow into a full stature is really what matters in practical life.

II

M. A.: What strikes me in the discussion we had before is that we are both on a level of conviction and belief. That is, I said that I had some sort of evidence that God exists. What is your evidence that He does not exist? On what do you base your belief?

M. L.: I think I've got to put it in a more negative way. I see no evidence that God exists. No reason to believe that God exists. What you take as evidence seems to me not to count as evidence, not to be sufficient evidence.

M. A.: You call that over-belief — ?

M. L.: Over-belief? I would say that undoubtedly you and people like you know a feeling that seems as if something that might be called God could exist, but this seems to me to be a feeling that something it might be useful to call God exists, not evidence that God exists. It seems to me more probably to be a feeling of it than true evidence.

M. A.: Where do you draw the line between evidence that is something that does exist and the superstructure which we'll call over-belief? How do you distinguish the one and the other?

M. L.: That is a difficult question, but I suppose that evidence would be something that if accepted as valid made a difference to one's entire mental patterning, something that had to be taken into account and which, if not taken into account, falsified every previous picture you'd held of how the world was, how it was constructed. I would rather find, I think, that to believe that God exists is supererogatory. Isn't it William of Occam who said you shouldn't multiply entities unnecessarily? I don't see a need to believe that God exists, or that if I did my picture of the world would be improved. In fact, I think my picture of the world would be falsified in that I would tend to make overtidy patterns about how things are if I believe that God exists, instead of confronting the much greater difficulties that seem to me to be there when I can't accept this.

M. A.: Yes, I see. But is an experience valid when it says to you God does exist? Can you invalidate that kind of statement?

M. L.: It doesn't seem to me to be a valid statement at all because there are all kinds of statements I can make from my experience. I can say at a moment of loving infatuation: 'This person is the person I shall be happy with all my life. He is the most beautiful, wonderful creature in the world.' But my eyes are blinded. Or I may have a fever and be hallucinated. Or the sun may shine and I may have an improper optimism about a situation. Or the sun may not shine and I may have an improper pessimism. Surely experience must be tempered by authority, just as authority must be tempered by experience, but on experience alone, I may be mad.

M. A.: That's the kind of thing which the atheists and the believers say about one another quite freely, so we can both accept that kind of qualification. But what is the basic difference between saying 'I know that God exists' and saying 'I know that love exists'?

M. L.: I don't think I would say 'I know that love exists' because I wouldn't use abstract words like this. I would say I know several different kinds of feelings that are called love, and it would be better, I think, if we restricted the word a bit more and used it for rather fewer feelings than rather many, but I can certainly say I know various feelings that people call love and I probably don't know all the feelings that people call love. For instance, I don't know your feeling of love of God in any adult sense.

M. A.: What if I simply denied the fact that love does exist, that there is such feeling—whatever the nuance you give it—I suppose you would say there is something lacking in me?

M. L.: But haven't you changed the words a bit? I say I know a feeling that it's reasonable to call love, just as I know a feeling of being right and a feeling of being wrong, but I wouldn't myself—I may be only quibbling with words—find it useful to say love exists, right exists, wrong exists. I know what it is to feel loving, let me put it that way, I know what it is when people are feeling loving towards me.

M. A.: Yes I see. But it's an irrational feeling, something which is pure feeling which you accept as an experience without assuming that at the back of it there is such a thing as love, as it were.

M. L.: No. You seem to be using irrational there as a rude word.

M. A.: On the contrary.

M. L.: But it's a feeling that has all kinds of validations hasn't it? I mean, for instance, you can observe my be-

haviour when I say I feel loving and say: 'Is my behaviour consonant with what counts as feeling loving?'
And if I say I am feeling loving when in fact my eyes are
glazed, my hands are cold, I have no energy, you would
then be justified in saying: 'Well she may call this love
but I think she's mad.' There are references for feeling
loving, aren't there?

M. A.: Yes. You moved from some sort of child's belief
into unbelief . . . or is it too personal a question, how did
you make the move from discarding God? Simply by the
fact that there was no evidence that satisfied your more
adult mind?

M. L.: Would you agree that a child's belief in God need
have very little to do with an adult's belief in God, except
when the adult comes to God he'll make a recognition?
This is what was presented to me as God when I was a
child and now I can see more clearly. I see that it was
right to present this to me. The God I knew and loved as
a child was a God presented to me by my parents and He
was an imaginary friend, as many children have, and I
think I had the same kind of belief in Him that I had,
say, in the fairies or that somewhere there was a country
called China. These were all things that came by authority
and had to stand the test of time.

M. A.: So it wasn't a God whom you would have said you
had met in a sort of intimate relationship. It was a God
whom someone else had met and about whom you had
been told?

M. L.: A little more than that because I think every
child's imaginary friend is somebody you meet in a per-

sonal relationship and I was certainly very convinced
that this God whom I loved was on my side, so to speak.
That when my parents said *this* was right and I thought,
no, *that* was right, God was with me not with them.

M. A.: You find, say in the Bible, in the Gospels in particular, a sort of poetic evidence but no sort of objective
evidence?

M. L.: No objective evidence of the existence of God but
an objective evidence of the kind of reasons that led
people to believe in God and, of course, a great many
statements of permanent validity without which I
couldn't live nearly so well as I try to.

M. A.: But do you think one can have convincing poetic
evidence which is founded on nothing but hallucination
or fantasy or wishful thinking?

M. L.: Now you are using rude words and unnecessarily
because it seems to me that religion would not have
existed in every community we know of unless it corres-
ponded to people's deepest needs which couldn't in other
ways be satisfied and when you say poetic, we in our post-
Renaissance world, take poetry as being something fairly
slight compared with religion. But I would have thought
that religion was the expression of something we had so
far no other means of expressing, something that is to do
with our whole best development as human beings. So
when I say I accept this as a poetic myth it's not to
denigrate it in fact it's rather greedily and jealously to
see what can I learn from it and in what ways human
beings can without the mythical basis of the myth still

continue to develop in a life that's a continuance from this and not a break from it.

M. A.: When I think of poetry as far as the human scene is concerned, I always feel that it carries weight, it makes sense because it is an expression in its own terms of something so profoundly real that poetry is the only medium which can be used to transmit the experience or to share it. But what makes it so convincing, so powerful is that there is a reality, human reality, at the root of it.

M. L.: But here we agree. I mean I think we were almost reaching the point of difference before . . . if you would say that poetry is an expression of a very deep human reality I am not away from you at all. It's when you suggest, if you are going to suggest, that there is something outside, something other, that we would disagree. It seems to me in fact that the subject of poetry, to take poetry literally now, that the subject that is most often used in poetry is the subject of this very deep emotional pattern-making, in some way closely related to a religious experience, that this is the thing poetry is most about.

M. A.: So that the human experience is genuine and the way it is interpreted you would feel is beyond the evidence as it were, the loss of words, imagination or fantasy.

M. L.: Beyond the evidence but not destructively beyond the evidence if one is able to accept it as mythical. We met before on television, I think a year ago, and I remember saying to you I understand you. I still believe that I understand you and I think perhaps this is what I am trying to say, that nothing that you put forward seems to me to be alien or strange but rather to be poetry in its deepest sense.

M. A.: And you would accept, for instance, that passages of the Gospel, to take the Gospel as an example, as being humanly true, without implying that it goes beyond the human truth of it?

M. L.: I would not only take them, I would seek them and use them.

M. A.: Because you mentioned the Lord's Prayer, for instance . . . What does the Lord's Prayer mean, apart from the God whom you call 'Our Father' in the beginning, or about Whose kingdom, will and so on you speak? Is it an incantation? You said that you used it.

M. L.: Yes, it's hard to say because its meaning changes from one pondering to another. You must find this too. And, except for using it as I think I do in a somewhat incantatory way, it wouldn't be perhaps the words that would most come to my lips, except for this purpose. I mean some of it I would accept, some I would reject. For instance: 'Lead us not into temptation' or, as it says in the New English Bible 'Do not bring us to the test.' This I would reject. This seems to me to be cowardly, but, on the other hand, the pious wish: 'Thy Kingdom Come' this seems an expression of Glory, this is splendid, this is life-giving.

M. A.: My difficulty is not so much such-and-such a sentence but the fact that the Lord's Prayer, for instance, is addressed to someone. If the someone doesn't exist at all, how does it affect you?

M. L.: I don't know the answer to that. I mean there is maybe still a childish recourse to a someone. I don't think there often is. Maybe I'm using your image. Could I produce another text, perhaps which I might find easier? One I often think of: 'I will lift up mine eyes to the hills from whence cometh my help.' Now this is more meaningful to me because the help that comes from looking at hills, to those of us who are helped by looking at hills, is a very real thing. We don't know, it may be, as people have said, something to do with the shape of the hills, whatever it may be, but I don't need then to assume a someone, a something that moves on the mountains. I just know, as a human being, that looking at hills is good for many human beings. It helps.

M. A.: I can't see that. My difficulty was that a prayer is addressed to someone or to a void and then I would feel that if there is a void towards which it is addressed then I couldn't use it.

M. L.: In moments of deep distress and disaster where it would be natural to pray, in that sense I can't pray, and this is one of the things we atheists must do without. I can see that it could be the greatest of strength and comfort to feel you could address a prayer and this perhaps is why I think people address prayers, but we can't do it.

M. A.: My feeling about it is not so much that there is someone to whom you can address a prayer but that the God who I believe exists, makes sense, and is a key of harmony even when the whole piece of music is totally discordant. Where is your key of harmony? Or is the world completely nonsensical?

M. L.: Perhaps there isn't a harmony but certainly I think that the attempt to impose a harmony goes far beyond anything we have a right to do, on what evidence we have. But we can seek for harmony in ourselves, harmony in our surroundings. We can seek the things that give us harmony. This I think is our duty. This is an important thing to do, but to say there is a great . . . a universal, an overall harmony, no, I think this is something we impose and God is one of the means by which we impose it.

M. A.: I won't say that there is one, but I would say that we are in a dynamic process of disharmony and tragedy that is aiming at and moving towards a final resolution, a meaning. How can you build meaning on the sort of patchwork which is life day by day?

M. L.: First, I wouldn't seek for anything in the nature of a final resolution because that would seem to me to be atrophy and death. The play, as you put it, of a movement towards tragedy and disorder, a movement towards harmony, is the very ebb and flow out of which creativity comes; but meaning, in any large sense, isn't something I would look for, no. I don't understand what this means.

M. A.: What do you feel of life then? You just exist, you act according to—I wouldn't say principles—but to promptings . . .

M. L.: Experience and authority—my experience, as purely as I can get it, the best authority I can find to try to be a good animal, a good human being, to the best of my capacity in my society, making as many choices as I feel it's in me to make, reconciling myself where I can't choose.

M. A.: And what about this scale of values? Is there such a thing as a scale of values between things bad and good, better or worse, ugliness and beauty? Is there any sort of base on which one can build a scale of values?

M. L.: I've got to be very simple here because what I go by is as easy as comes. What makes me feel better is good. What makes me feel worse is bad. But authority must come in. You see, again, I could be mad. I could be a sadist. If I feel better at beating a child then I must defer to authority. There's something wrong with me, I should go to a doctor. But what makes me feel better, in society, as a social animal, I think, if tested by authority—and part of the authority I could certainly use would be the authority of religion—what tends towards health, the health of me in my society, is good. What tends to un-health is bad.

M. A.: Yes, but health and unhealth are very relative notions.

M. L.: Need they be? Just as you, as a doctor, as you have been, can recognise a state of greater or lesser physical health. Surely we are moving towards a point where we are able to recognise a larger kind of health than that, a health . . a social health for instance of a community, a psychosomatic health of the individual as a whole; and one of the things we should be able to do in ourselves, and always with this check of authority, is to know what's good for us, and the word good is quite important there, to know what's bad for us.

M. A.: What troubles me is for instance that in the case where the physical well-being of people has improved, they feel happier, and yet often I feel so sorry for them because they are missing something more important, and I would rather be back to more misery but be alive in the way I was than be more stable, more happy, more satisfied and less dynamically alive.

M. L.: I don't think this is wiped out by what I've said. Are you saying better Socrates dissatisfied than the pig satisfied? I think the polarity between unhappiness and happiness, between ill-health and good health, between stagnation and movement, all this is what makes for movement and creativity. And so the last thing I would be saying is what I want to be in a state of perfect endless bliss because this would be similar to your final harmony. You know the atheist poet, William Cory, who said: 'Your chilly heavens I can forgo, this warm, kind world is all I know,' and the chilly heavens do indeed seem to me to be the area of cold movementlessness like an icy sea.

M. A.: I don't think that harmony is bound to be stagnation or immobility. When, for instance, you spin a top, there is a moment when the movement is so perfect and intense that it coincides with complete poise.

M. L.: But your harmony—I mean if we are talking about music—the harmony of music is made by playing on your nerves, by the exacerbation of discords, by the expectation that isn't fulfilled. There's no peace but the grave.

M. A.: True, there is no peace but the grave, but I don't see harmony as a grave. What do you think of the people who are sure that there is an otherness which they call God, how do you take into account their experience or what they assert? Do you think that all of them were completely mistaken in their judgement or hallucinated?

M. L.: You lead me to the besetting sin of the atheist which is arrogance, so I think I have to say I don't know. I guess there to be a temperamental difference. I guess there to be a difference between people who prefer a minuscule putting together of pieces that may never reach a whole and people like Plato, perhaps, who saw a perfection in ideals. There do seem to me to be people who yearn for an otherness and people who yearn for a here and now, and this is not to make judgement between them but to say that perhaps it's something to do with the way your brain works.

M. A.: Yes, but you spoke of authority as one of the bases for decision and thought. If you take the total authority of mankind in the sense that they occupy a place which seems to be discordant with another line, with the line you have taken, do you feel you need integrate them somehow or would you say, as an atheist once said to me: 'Your belief comes either from hopeless ignorance, or, from the fact that you are a crack-pot and as you are not hopelessly ignorant'—or rather he thought I was hopeless but he didn't think I was sufficiently ignorant—'then you must be a hopeless crack-pot.'

M. L.: When I said authority I wasn't thinking again of authority for a great big thing, but for little things. 'The hedgehog knows one big thing and the fox knows many things.' I'm a fox. You're a hedgehog. So when I refer to authority, I want to know what authority has said about charity, what authority has said about adultery, what authority has said about lies and anger. But not what it's said about God. It simply seems to me that where these human problems are concerned, what should I do? How should I behave? How can I find consolation? The Fathers of the Church and the Fathers of the Synagogue have been into all this and they've found answers that suit human beings, so there is likely to be an answer that suits me. I don't have to take the source of their answer, but their answer is very likely to suit my condition.

M.A.: I find it surprising because in our time particularly people are so interested in knowing all that exists — travelling and having seen, having read, having heard, being aware of the total reality. My question about this reality is that I feel God is perhaps part of this reality or is not, and it's not immaterial to know whether He exists any more than it is immaterial to know whether something else of the material world exists. It's as important in a way, not for a world outlook, but for the sake of my passionate interest in what there is.

M.L.: But I have said I don't think God exists. How would my life be changed if I thought otherwise? How would my very imperfect world picture be made more perfect, how would my life be different?

M.A.: What is the difference for your life to have discovered that music exists? In a way, you could very well live without ever having had any experience of music. It may not have made you any better, any worse, but it's an enrichment. It is part of a real and wider experience of life and that's how I would put the problem about God.

M.L.: I see this. But surely God doesn't exist for my enrichment. You're suggesting almost that there's another art form I haven't come across. I'm tone deaf to God and I would have a richer life if I wasn't, just as I might if I could understand another art that I don't understand. But God must be something more than this.

M. A.: And yet, as far as my human experience is concerned, when in times past I've said: 'I've no use for music, I am not interested and I dislike it,' people have said: 'Oh poor one. You miss so much and you are short of part of life.'

M. L.: But at least you knew that music existed. You could watch us listening to it. You could see these people scraping away.

M. A.: With great thought and meditation . . . But what about us scraping away? What about, say, the great people like St Theresa?

M. L.: I don't go greatly for St Theresa, because it seems to me that whenever she didn't find people who would agree with her exact interpretation of God, she sought for another adviser, so she is not my favourite saint. But I think she's a good example because she, more than most people, actually believed she perceived God beyond the point which Christianity allows in fact, and yet she did not really submit her visions to authority. As I say, she changed her authority whenever it didn't suit her vision.

M. A.: Yet here is a woman and here are many people who possess something they say is real. And you would go a long way to discover a new writer, a new artist, in terms of painting or sculpture, a new world of discovery, and yet you would say this is not worth investigating and discovering. That's what puzzles me.

M.L.: I don't think I'm saying that. I would certainly probably not have investigated it so far as you would think proper. It's certain that I don't see any substitute for this world of yours because since the Renaissance for instance, it's been all too sadly apparent that in all the arts there has been no inspiration comparable with the inspiration that religion gave. There have been no words for secular music that compare with the music of a Mass. I certainly think that belief in God and the religions that arose from belief in God did give a shaping and a pattern to life for which I can see no conceivable substitute, and to that extent I would certainly grant to you that my life is poorer than that of a believer. My justification for it, and I say it as humbly as I can, is that it's founded on the truth as I see it and the truth has to make me free of perfection. I'm not entitled to it.

M.A.: I feel terribly happy about what you said because I think what really matters first of all is integrity and truth and I'm certain that if God exists, which I believe He does, He's happier about truth of unbelief than falsified belief. Now I think I must give you the chance you gave me to say what you would like to say in addition to our discussion.

M.L.: I probably haven't made atheism seem at all rich and I don't think it is. I think it's a very Protestant, a very puritanical faith that, as I say, does tend towards arrogance because we lack authority. But there is one thing I would say for atheism, as against religion, and that is this: if you try to practise it, it trains you in a virtue that I value highly which is endurance without whimpering and without seeking help you can't properly expect to have. But we must—I say 'we', I don't know who 'we' are, I don't know who atheists are and this is, again, where arrogance comes in—but we must depend very deeply on religions which have a great many things that we can't have—rite, ritual, festival, words beyond any words we've managed to maintain. I think sometimes that we could have more help.

CHAPTER TWO

DOUBT AND DISCLOSURE

Periodically words emerge that characterise a situation. When one uses the words 'problem' and 'problematic', one means things that had seemed to be absolutely clear to the generation before but which have now unfolded themselves in a new way and have acquired a depth of vision which requires new thinking. We are no longer content with a simple repetition of views which belonged to a previous generation. I am talking about such things as the historical meaning of tragic events like the Russian Revolution, suffering—communal or family—and national tragedies.

Nowadays it seems that the words which come easily to mind are *bewilderment, perplexity,* and they result in an attitude of mind because the trouble with words is that they begin by defining a situation that exists and then they tend to crystallise the situation, making out of it a sort of world outlook. People confronted with a problem are perplexed; they say so, and that is right. Later, however, people have come to the perplexity before the problem and think that they are up to date if they are perplexed—but that doesn't always lead to a solution.

Therefore, before we start to consider anything more concrete in our faith or world outlook, I would like to focus attention on perplexity and on doubt, in an attempt to provoke thought about a few words like faith, doubt, reality and truth. I am not a theologian; I am a scientist by training and a physician, so you will not find in my words any depth of philosophical probing into things. I am writing as an ordinary human being who is confronted with life and its problems.

First of all, concerning faith, one preliminary remark. Faith is very often understood by people as a defeat of intelligence. In other words, faith begins when I can no longer think creatively, when I let go of any attempt at rational understanding, and when I say 'I believe' because it is so absurd that it is the only way of facing the problem. This may be an act of credulity, it may be an act of cowardice, it may be a preliminary act, full of wisdom and intelligence, that teaches us not to come to conclusions before we have understood. But this is not faith as understood by the great men of all religions, and particularly the Christian faith. In the Epistle to the Hebrews in the eleventh chapter, faith is defined as the 'certainty of things unseen'. We usually lay the stress on 'things unseen' and forget the 'certainty' about them. So when we think of faith we usually think of the invisible and instead of certainty put against it an interrogation mark. Then to solve the problem, we accept in a childish way, in an unintelligent way very often, what we are told by others—usually our grandparents of three generations back, or anyone else we choose to believe for reasons that are not always reasonable.

But if you try to see the way in which faith originates in those people who were the great men of faith, the heroes of faith, you can see that it always originates in an experience that makes the *invisible certain*, and which allows them, having discovered that the invisible is as real as the visible, to go further in searching the invisible by methods of their own. There is a passage for instance, in the works of Makarios of Egypt, a man who lived in the fourth century. He says that the experience of God, the vision of the world in God, is something which can happen only at a moment when all our thoughts, all our emotions, are arrested to such a degree that we can no longer both be within the experience, perceive the things, and step out of the experience, watch ourselves and analyse what is going on. The moment when an experience is 'lived' is a moment when we cannot observe it. And he says that this would be quite sufficient for someone who has had an experience of God. He would not wish to go back to another stage. But he also says that God has concern, not only for those who have this experience, but also for the people who have not; in order that someone should come to them as a witness of things unseen, and yet experienced, real, He steps back from him. At that moment begins, as he says, the realm of faith. The certitude remains even though the experience is already of the past; the certainty is there because what has happened to him is as certain as anything around him, tangible, visible, perceived by the senses, so that the moment of faith begins as a result of a first contact with the invisible, discovered, disclosed to him.

That means that we must be very severe and sober when we speak of our faith, for we often say 'I believe this and that' when we have taken that it is true from someone else—we don't care to investigate it in depth, and as long as this truth or illusory truth is not challenged, then we take it for granted. This is a poor faith; this is what one of our Russian theologians called 'the eighth sacrament of the faith that does not think'. What we should do whenever we are faced with that kind of faith is to confront it with experience. We must ask ourselves whether we have any experience of it. If we haven't, it must remain a field to be investigated. It remains a field that was conveyed to us by someone who knows, but which is not known to us. It is promising, but it must hold its promise in the future. We cannot yet say 'I know, I am certain, I understand with experience.'

This kind of faith—the faith of one who simply takes things on trust—will sooner or later be badly battered by life and by problems, by doubt, by perplexity in fact. What happens so often with people is that when they are young, they are given a number of certainties which they accept on trust from their parents, their teachers, the milieu in which they live. After that, this minimum of faith is kept as a sort of treasure. We develop in all sorts of ways, but our awareness of the world invisible and of the certainties it entails does not grow with it. A moment comes around the age of eighteen, perhaps earlier or later, when the child in us, the little child of eight who has collected all the faith he was capable of and formed a world outlook which is childish, is confronted with an opponent, an adversary within, a young adult who says 'Nonsense, you can't believe that.' Then an argument starts which is doomed to lead to the defeat of faith simply because it is the argument between a little child with a pure heart and unevolved thinking, against someone who poses to the childish nature the problems of another age, another level of understanding, another level of perception of the world.

At eight the world can be taken on trust; at eighteen it cannot; and in certain circumstances there are things that can never be taken on trust. I will give you an example. The Eucharist, the central event of Christian worship, is based on an act of thanksgiving in which we say to God 'Thank you for all things.' Now, can we honestly say, 'thank you for all things' in the face of the tragedies of the world unless we have a reason to see beyond the tragedy to their solution and a meaning within them?

Doubt is not simply contradiction. Doubt is a moment of dividedness, a dichotomy in our minds; a moment when, having followed a very simple straight road, we come to a fork, and we ask ourselves 'Do I go this way or that way?' The one may be more convincing, the other may be more alluring. Which one are we going to choose? It is the situation of someone who has been weighing up the problems of life in a very simple way and suddenly discovers there is a much more subtle balance between things and that a simple solution is no solution at all. What are we going to do at that moment?

There are two quite different attitudes to doubt— there is that of the scientist and that of the believer. For the scientist, doubt is a systematic weapon; it is a joy. For the believer when he takes the wrong attitude to doubt and to the problems he is facing, it is a moment of anguish. What happens usually to the believer is that having believed in all simplicity that everything is clear, simple, straightforward, he suddenly discovers that life gives the lie to what he thought to be true. Then his answer is 'I am disloyal to what I thought, I am disloyal to my faith, to my Church, to my God.' The problem is not only about subtleties but about basic things, about God Himself, about the Church, about what is at the core of the believer's life. Then he feels that what is at stake is the collapse, the destruction, the disappearance of the *object of faith*, that God's existence is now questionable. The values which were essential, which were existential values for him, are questionable, and therefore his very existence becomes a seemingly insuperable problem.

But when a scientist engages in research, he gathers together all the facts he is capable of collecting. Once he has gathered them, he must hold them together in a way that makes it possible for him to handle the totality of the facts, and he builds a hypothesis, a theory, a model that is capable of holding everything together. If the whole object of research for the scientist is to make himself a name, he will try to protect his model against any criticism, against any doubt and against any questioning, with greater or lesser honesty. But if as a scientist he is a man who is out to discover what things are in reality, his first action will be to go round and round his model in all directions, examining and trying to find where the flaw is, what the problems are which are generated by the model he has built, by the theory he has proposed, by the hypothesis he has now offered for the consideration of others. If he cannot find a flaw, then he will try through research to go farther in the field and discover such facts as do not fit with his theory or his model, because when he finds a fact that will expose his model, make his theory questionable, he will have opened up a new window on reality. So the aim of the good research scientist is to create models or theories or hypotheses as a preliminary exercise to questioning and to discovering something which will make him break them down, in order to create another model which is as dubitable as the preceding one, but which allows him to keep the new facts together in a manageable way.

At the root of the scientist's activity there is the certainty that what he is doubting is the model he has invented—that is, the way in which his intelligence has grouped things. But what he is also absolutely certain of is that the reality which is beyond his model is in no danger if his model collapses. The reality is stable, it is there; the model is an inadequate expression of it, but the reality doesn't alter because the model fails.

'Model' can be replaced by another word when it is not used in a scientific way—it can be replaced by the word

'truth'. Truth is something which is an expression of
reality, and an expression means two things: first, that
the reality which surrounds us is perceived (obviously
incompletely); secondly, that it is expressed (also incompletely, because of our inability to express reality in exact
words and expressions). Only *one* occasion in human history sees the moment when truth and reality coincide.
That moment is the Incarnation: Christ, because He is
God, the plenitude, the fullness of creation, and at the
same time the perfect expression of it. Then truth no
longer answers the question 'What?', it answers the question 'Who?', and when Pilate said 'What is truth?' Christ
gave him no answer, for the simple reason that if He had
said to him what He had said to the disciples, 'I am the
Truth' Pilate would have understood even less than the
disciples, and the disciples understood little at that particular moment.

Truth is bound to be formulated in human terms, in
the language of a given tribe, a nation, an epoch and so
forth. Obviously it is limited, but it has also another
quality: truth can be either static or dynamic. You can
express the truth in two ways. A snapshot is true and yet
it is perfectly untrue. Everyone must have seen pictures
of preachers, lecturers or politicians delivering a speech.
They are usually taken at a moment when the subject
stands with his mouth open like a hippopotamus. Well,
the picture is perfectly true, but it expresses only a split
second and gives you a ridiculous image of something that
perhaps at that moment was profoundly moving for the
listeners. It is a petrification, a sort of fossil of something
which is dynamic; it is true, and yet it does not express
the truth because the truth at that moment was movement. When you want to be true to reality — dynamically,
you discover that the truth becomes a problem of a quite

different sort. Perhaps an example or two will explain what I mean.

There is a painting by the French painter Géricault called *The Derby at Epsom*. If you look at the painting, you will see that the horses are galloping, but if you are interested in zoology or in the mechanics of movement and examine the horses, you will discover that no horse gallops that way. Some are spread out in such a way that if they went on they would fall flat on their bellies; others stand with their four feet gathered together and couldn't even jump from the position in which they are painted. But what was Géricault aiming at? He aimed at showing the gallop and not the horses. The problem was to express the movement and not the anatomy. And he chose deliberately (because he knew perfectly well how to draw a horse) to falsify things as the only way of convincing the viewer that the horses were moving.

This is what we are always doing in theology or philosophy: we falsify things when we want to convey a dynamic moment, but often the reader takes them to be an adequate and immobile picture of what reality is. This applies, for instance, to the dynamic relationship of the Trinity.

There is another example which I should like to give about reality. It is that of false teeth. When we say these are false teeth, we are making a judgement of value but not of reality. We start with the common assumption that real teeth grow spontaneously in peoples' mouths. This is true; from this point of view those teeth which you can remove in the evening, wash under the tap and keep in a glass are evidently false. But from the point of view of the dentist, they are perfectly real (false) teeth. It sounds like a joke, but that is the kind of mistake which we make continually. We don't notice it, but we start to speak of something from one angle, move to another and we discover that the two don't work together.

No, reality is something within us which is the total thing which includes God and all things visible and invisible. This is what we aim at expressing in glimpses when we speak in terms of truth. These terms of truth may be adequate, they are never identical with their object.

In the field of art something very interesting may be discovered in the works of primitive painters such as the Russian ikon painter called Rublev, who lived 600 years ago. He was trained by a man who was a master of three-dimensional painting, and strangely enough, for most of his painting he reverted to two-dimensional forms. A Soviet historian of art made a study of the problem, and he showed that Rublev expresses all historical events in three-dimensions, because particularly in time and space they have thickness. But things which belong to the eternal, he expresses only in two dimensions because they have no thickness—they are not within time and within space. When you look out of the window during the night in a thunderstorm, you may see the scenery in a flash—but it goes so quickly that you can't see whether one tree is farther or nearer than another, or any such precise detail. This is the way that truth is both adequate and inadequate. When we say that the truth is inadequate, that our intellectual, philosophical, theological, scientific model is inadequate in comparison with reality, it simply means that we are saying 'How marvellous, I have come to a point when I can outgrow the limitations in which I have lived and I can move into a greater, deeper, more enthralling vision of things as they are.'

If we think of a scientist and a believer, then we will see

that the scientist's doubt is systematic, it presses onward, it is hopeful, it is joyful, it is destructive of what he has done himself, because he believes in the reality that is beyond and not in the model he has constructed. This we must learn as believers for our spiritual life both in the highest forms of theology and in the small simple concrete experience of being a Christian. Whenever we are confronted with a crossroads, whenever we are in doubt, whenever our mind sees two alternatives, instead of saying 'Oh God, make me blind, Oh God help me not to see, Oh God give me loyalty to what I know now to be untrue,' we should say 'God is casting a ray of light which is a ray of reality on something I have outgrown—the smallness of my original vision. I have come to a point when I can see more and deeper, thanks be to God.' That is not perplexity, it is not bewilderment, it is not the anguished doubt of the believer who hides his head and hopes that he will be able to revert to the age of eight.

This is very important because unless you are prepared to see reality and your own thoughts and the thoughts of others with keen interest, with courage, but with the certainty that the last word is not doubt, not perplexity and not bewilderment, but that it is *discovery*, then you are wasting your time. You will perish in the same way as the ass we are told about in ancient mythology that stood between a bucket of water and some straw and could never decide whether he was more hungry than thirsty or more thirsty than hungry.

There is an expression which was particularly dear to Ian Ramsey, the late Bishop of Durham. Many do not immediately understand what it means, but then discover that it has a depth of meaning and serves a very useful purpose. The expression is 'cosmic disclosure'. Cosmic disclosure means that there are moments when things which surround us—people, situations—suddenly acquire depth, become transparent, as it were, and allow us to see them with a new significance, and as I said, with depth. The nearest approximation to cosmic disclosure I could give you is something which we probably all know about. When I was small I was given a little drawing made up of a maze of lines. What you could distinguish at once in this maze of lines was a hunter in a wood, and the caption said 'Where is the rabbit?' Then you took the thing and began to look at it this way and that way in all directions, until suddenly you saw the rabbit and you couldn't understand how it was that you hadn't seen it before.

That is true as an image for everything in life. We live in a situation, with people, we see the situation at its face value, we see people apparently as they are, and one day we suddenly spot something else. How great, how profoundly significant that is! That happens, for instance, when we look at very familiar scenery one day when we are perceptive, when we have eyes to see, and are capable of response. We look at the most ordinary thing which we have seen day after day, and suddenly we stand arrested by beauty, by meaning, by something it lends us, as though things had become translucent and we could see in depth, deeper and deeper towards a core that is full of meaning.

The same happens with people. We live among people and we see them as people. People are interchangeable in the crowd, faces move and there is always a face to be seen. But all of a sudden a face that we have often seen, which has become so familiar that we don't even look at it any more because from the first glimpse we know that's him or that's her—suddenly we have stopped to look, or because something in the eyes, something in the expression has made us stop. The face appears to us completely new, lending us a depth of meaning, a depth of significance. And someone who was an interchangeable part of the crowd is singled out in such a way that he becomes a person, and a person who is unique, who can't be replaced by any other person, can't be confused, is simply himself or herself.

There is a saying of Methodius Olympius, a Greek divine, that 'As long as we don't love a person, one person, we are surrounded with men and women. The moment our heart has discovered the person it loves there is the beloved one and nothing but people around.' This is the way in which something can be singled out, seen in depth and in truth—seen, I was about to say, in glory, because in those moments things which were lifeless, colourless or dull, suddenly acquire relief, colour, beauty and meaning. In such moments occurs what Ian Ramsey calls 'cosmic disclosure'. That kind of cosmic disclosure we all know, and if we are attentive to ourselves we will remember such moments—moments when suddenly, among people whom we know very well, we discover someone, with a warmth of heart, with a vision, with an emotion we never had before. A thought that has been repeatedly thrust at us in the form of quotation from the Gospel or from literature, which somehow clicks in a situation and acquires deep meaning, is no longer a quotation from Shakespeare or from the Scriptures; it is *truth* that has been put into words which are so significant and so powerful.

This kind of experience is akin to the experience which we have of God because God is also someone whom we can discover in this moment of cosmic disclosure. I insist on the word 'cosmic' this time because God is within the reality in which we live, and furthermore, as long as we have not discovered Him and the invisible world that is

His world, we are still blind to a whole wealth of reality. This is why it is important, from my point of view, to have discovered God. In a way I would say it is rather a danger, very often a nuisance. One could very well live with less trouble without a God than with a God because —particularly with a God who has accepted solidarity to the point of death, love to the point of forgetting Himself and in addition to this, is vulnerable, helpless, despised, beaten—God tells us coldbloodedly: this is the example which I give you—follow it. Or He says, here are the beatitudes: you will be hungry, you will be thirsty, you will be beaten, you will be cast out, you will be persecuted—and that is the best you can have. That kind of God is not always a discovery that brings ease in our lives. The point is not whether God will be useful, the point is whether it is true that He exists.

Now, can one attach any validity, to this kind of cosmic disclosure which includes beauty, love, human relationships, the existence of God, and a new vision of the world? What is the validity of experience? There is a point of view which I believe to be a falsification of a scientific approach that says: experience is something that can be proved according to methods of natural science or the exact sciences like physics, chemistry, biology. This, I think, is a falsification because experience is not limited to that kind of science. There is a whole world which is irrational, yet not unreasonable. When I was a student and studied physics, I had to pass the exam on acoustics. I was totally uninterested in music and totally incapable of appreciating it at all. To me, music was a sequence of sounds. I knew all about music as far as sound was concerned and as far as physics was involved; as to enjoying it—no, it never occurred to me that it was enjoyable. I knew a man who took the same line about literature—a very remarkable man I met in Ireland, an old canon who was the shyest and the most reserved creature I have ever met and who found the English extraordinary and so unbearably exuberant that he could not stand a holiday in Britain because he came back exhausted. He asked me once whether I knew Dostoevsky. I was rather surprised that he was interested in Dostoevsky and I said, 'Have you read him? How do you like his novels?' He looked at me and said, 'Novels? I never thought he wrote novels.' I said, 'What did you read then?' He mentioned all Dostoevsky's well-known works. I asked 'What were you looking for?' It turned out that he was collecting a card index on Russian religion and he had read the whole of Dostoevsky but had never noticed that he was a novelist. It takes a 'cosmic disclosure' to change this!

There is such a thing as the irrational that cannot be simply reduced to rational formulae. We know now that there is a whole world of the irrational in us which is not the realm of intellect and reason, yet which exists and has immense power in us. Emotional troubles are not rational and yet they are more decisive in our total balance than our points of view, when in an Olympian way, that is, with total indifference, we view things. But there is another thing about the kind of experience which people would advocate, saying 'That is reliable, I have probed into it with my five senses.' But our five senses are no more reliable than any kind of inner reaction. When you look at something, you say: I am sure it is there; my eyes give me evidence. When I listen to something, I say: I am sure it is there; my ears have given me evidence. But what is the evidence? I remember very well a patient once, who sat next to me and as I was talking to her she suddenly began to pat thin air. I said 'Oh, what's that?' And the good lady said, 'It's an ethereal lion. I live in an astral body and not only in a physical body, and I have a nice little lion that comes and sits with me.' This good lady felt the lion's fur under her hand; she could see the lion; I couldn't I'm afraid. Now, from my point of view her physical perception of the lion was a hallucination; from her point of view the reason for my lack of perception was my denseness and my blindness. With everything we see, we assume first of all that previous experience is proof that it is true, and secondly we pass a judgement of value, that this is not hallucination and that it is reality. From the point of view of natural life, of course we may be right or wrong, but from the point of view of psychological thinking, I have a right to challenge and to doubt any visual, audible, sensory experience because your eyes are not the part of you that assert that this is a lion or that this is a watch. It is your judgement, your head, your brains that say that. And between the lion that sits here and your eyes that catch sight of him in his absence and the nervous system that brings it to your brain and your brain that takes cognisance of it and your judgement that says it is a real lion and not a fantasy, is a nice long chain which I can doubt at more than one link.

One can show experimentally that many of the things which we assume so easily are more doubtful than we imagine. So that unless we are prepared, as philosophers or scientists have been to doubt systematically any experience we have, there is no logical, solid reason to question one type of experience and admit of the other, especially when a type of experience is not the experience of one unique person, but when it is corroborated by the experience, the practical knowledge of other people.

So the fact that an experience will not be transmitted directly or cannot be given evidence to by what we call objective methods is proof of nothing, because the words *objective* and *subjective* must be treated with a great deal more care. An objective judgement usually means a judgement which I can pass with total indifference, without any kind of prejudice, and in practice that's what we mean by this. But if we want to have an objective vision of something, what we should really mean is that we must perceive the thing as the thing perceives itself without interfering. That is obviously totally impossible; I cannot perceive a chair by identifying myself with the chair. But I do perceive something when something happens to me. As long as it remains only the object and unrelated to me, there is no perception at all, not to speak of any kind of experience. I think we must take that into account, because neither in music, nor in physics, nor in any kind of rational and precise science, is there objectivity that does not involve a subject. And if that is true, then all the complex experiences of beauty, of love, of appreciation, of evaluation of judgement, of inner certainty which we can have, have an objective significance for another person.

Now this is important because unless we understand this, we must deny systematically any experience which is not tangible and we can doubt any experience which is tangible, unless we accept a total interplay of immutable laws of identity in the outside world and in the laws of nature which modern science can no longer admit in the crude and simplified way of, say, the eighteenth and nineteenth centuries.

There is another problem. In this intercourse between subjective and objective there are two things. First of all, an experience which has become mine, I must be able to retain, to examine and express; on the other hand, others must be able to receive it, that is, to receive the message of it. You cannot retain an experience by memorising it.

We say in Russia that after a meal you cannot understand the hungry; you cannot imagine what it means to be hungry or thirsty or tired when you are no longer these things. You cannot memorise, in terms of emotion, an experience—if you try, you will only fake your feelings. Things are retained by their association with something outside ourselves, something which stimulates our mind or our senses. Don't you know what happens to you when you have been in a place where you were happy or miserable and come back after ten years and suddenly the same sunlight, the same house, the same situation—how, in a flash, all the emotions of ten years ago well up in you which you could not have conjured up by an act of intellectual imagination?

Remember the story of Jeremiah. He was shown by God, one day, a twig of almond tree, and God spoke to him at the same time and said, 'What do you see?' The answer was 'God is the keeper of Israel.' This is built on a grammatical pun in the Hebrew language which is irrelevant for what we need now. But can you imagine the state in which Jeremiah was? He saw the twig of almond tree and all of a sudden he was overwhelmed with the sense of the Divine Presence. Don't you think that whenever he held in his hand a twig of almond tree, he was brought back to that much more than by any sort of theological reminiscence?

When we wish to convey an experience that we have had to other people, there are two ways of doing it. Firstly, we can put someone in the situation of gaining for himself the experience we wish to share. If we want someone to know a work of Beethoven or Mozart we would not sit him down and make a long discourse about harmony and counterpoint. We would say, 'They are playing Beethoven tonight, come and listen'—receive the impact of it, live through it, let it live in you.

The other way is the way of all literature; by analogy, by metaphor and image, in which we start with something the person knows that helps him to make what one calls in physics and mathematics an extrapolation—to draw conclusions beyond the experience, and thanks to that to outgrow, to extend one's knowledge. For instance, when we speak of love; we know it has many forms and that they are not identical—a little girl of seven will never understand what it means that her teenage sister is madly in love, because there is analogy but not identity of experience. But through an analogical experience one can catch a glimpse of another's. That is what happens when we have suffered real suffering or known real joy. We can understand the suffering and the joy of others—not by suffering their suffering or rejoicing their joy—but by compassion, suffering together, rejoicing with them, with understanding.

The seers, the visionaries, those who know by experience the certainty of things invisible, try to express things in words that are usually ordinary words, to impart something that would make sense to us.

Take for instance that night in Jerusalem when Nicodemus came to see the Lord. You can imagine the scene. They probably stood on the terrace of the house to talk in the evening breeze instead of remaining in the stuffy heat indoors. They were speaking of God, invisible, intangible, Who cannot be caught in any kind of net. Nicodemus didn't understand and Christ said 'Look, what do you perceive now? You perceive the wind blowing around us, your skin is refreshed, your clothes are stirring in the air. It is an actuality, a certainty that you are within this refreshing, life-giving, blowing of the evening breeze. Yet you do not know where it comes from, you do not know where it goes. You know nothing about it except this complete personal experience that makes you say an objective thing: "The wind is blowing, I am refreshed".'

Forms of speech, methods of expression will change with the semantics of a language, with the epoch in which they are spoken, with the context in which they are used, what one calls very often 'situation theology', until you come to formulations of a few words which contain—as in a nutshell—a kernel that is so tiny, dry and compact, yet holds *life* within itself, and which, if you will let it take root in you, will begin to disclose to you a vision of life that will enable you to grow into what you are called to be.

CHAPTER THREE

MAN AND GOD

In the eighteenth and nineteenth centuries, the centre of interest was mainly ideas and ideals, and man was the material support of these ideals or these concepts. He was subservient to them, he was supposed to serve them, to live for them and eventually to die for them. There was greatness in this approach and if we forget its significance, we would certainly lose a very important dimension of humanity. Man's greatness is I believe, to be measured, not only by his potentialities but also by his ability to live and die for things which in his view are greater than he is. But we know also that when ideals and ideas acquire such power as to become overlords of the minds and lives of people, when men are no longer free to approach them critically, but are forced into a mould that involves them in life and death without any choice of their own, then something has gone wrong. And it is not surprising that nowadays, as a revulsion against what has been happening since the beginning of the First World War, we have a sense of the value and the significance of man in his frailty, in his becoming, in his search, as well as in his achievements and in the service he can render to things great. It is even true that in our time the value of man is so much to the fore, and in such a peculiar way, that doubt is sometimes thrown on the value of ideas. There is certainly exaggeration in this; an equilibrium has to be found between the value of man and that to which he gives his life and dedicates his death. But none the less it is true that in the mentality of today, both within and without the Church, man plays an essential role. He is not simply an object or instrument destined to accomplish works, nor is he the unique bearer of an idea. Man is seen to be more complex, he appears as a reality too rich to be reduced to the singleness of an ideology.

Nowadays *Man* is a meeting point of all those who are in search of things true and things right. If St Paul came back into our world and was faced with an altar dedicated to the Unknown God, he might very well say 'I know his name, his name is Man', and at that point he would probably meet not only those who believe but also those whom we call the unbelievers. Man is now a point of real and extremely fruitful encounter between those who hold the two most clearly opposing ideologies: faith and atheism. Man is the only object which they have in common. I would like to build part of this chapter on two quotations: one belongs to Karl Marx and the other to St John Chrysostom. They are two poles whose axis is man. Marx says that the proletariat has no need of a god because man has become his god. And St John Chrysostom declares: 'If you want to measure the greatness of man, raise your eyes towards the throne of God and you will see the Word Incarnate, the Son of Man, the bearer of our humanity, seated at the right hand of the Glory.' Here are the two clearest expressions of the modern situation. In both cases it is man who is the final, the greatest vision and greatest value.

I would like to take up not these two quotations themselves, but the vision of man which they imply, and see whether the atheist and the Christian have anything to say to one another about it. For the atheist world—I mean the atheist world that has an ideology, not the atheist world of the stomach which one might call 'gastric' atheism, about whom St Paul is speaking when he tells us, 'These men's god is their belly'—for the ideological atheist who bases himself on that conception of the world, theoretical man is truly a god. The striking thing is that, on the one hand, the theoretical man is a god; at the same time the empirical man is a victim and a slave. This, I think, is explained by the fact that the theoretical man who is placed on the altar of atheism is not a personal man, he is not each man considered in his person, inimitable and unique, but the collective man. And this theoretical-collective man, who is unique, challenges the rights of the individual man. The former is the man of the present and the future; not the concrete man living in the present or the individual man who will live in the future, but humanity—or the 'class'—and this is always a collectivity which has the right to make absolute demands on each of its members. In the matter of art, literature, civic conduct and conscientious inner conviction, this collectivity has totalitarian claims. And the concrete man, the individual, has only his small place in it: he cannot go beyond the place assigned to him; he only has the right to possess, like a tiny piece of mosaic, cut, shaped, adjusted to fit, the position and colour that are imposed upon him. The concrete man is raw material; this raw material is in the process of *becoming*; from the point of view of natural science it would be called evolution, from the point of view of social science one would speak of an evolving society, but the empirical man is not *the* reality which concerns the atheist uniquely. As raw material he exists, but he is to be set up against a certain number of visions, the first of which may be of the man of the future—man when he will have become what he should be. I remember a discussion I had on a plane between Moscow and the south of Russia with an atheist who said to me that we should not judge the success or failure of the Russian Revolution by what was actually achieved or not achieved as yet, because the result of the revolution will be shown when men will have been transformed in such a way that they become real men. In other words, man is always viewed as something ahead, something in the future towards which we move; and the empirical raw material which we all are is to be worked upon, transformed, changed and remoulded, and in this recasting, as experience shows through the centuries, many bones crack and many things have to be changed by force and even violence.

In the case of society defining man or in the case of an ideal abstract man being set up as the pattern for the future, we always meet—whatever the case, whatever the kind of dictatorship or pressure group—with something which the Russian writer, Solzhenitsyn, in his book *Cancer Ward*, defined in the following way. One of the central characters has this said about him, 'He had the greatest possible love and consideration for mankind, and this is why he hated so fiercely every human being because they disfigured this ideal so horribly.' This is exactly what happens when we have no other standard and no other point of reference than either an ideal which we build out of our imagination according to what we desire, or else when society, the pack around us, defines what each of the howling wolves should be. Man confronted with an abstract ideal of man or with a concrete, real society which claims totalitarian rights, must be remoulded, must be broken, must be changed and must be brought—a blood offering very often—to this abstract ideal or perish, for he does not fit in with the pack, the concrete society, the jungle in which he lives.

Christianity also sets man as the final value, but not idealistically or abstractly.

There is in the Church a vision of man which is not a theory of man. It is not the ideal man, it is not the invented man, nor man as we wish he were, and towards which we aim as a sort of created transcendence. No, we have put on the altar a concrete real man—Jesus of Nazareth—and we must have a look at what is implied. We see in the Creed that Christ was true man and true God. When we say that He was true man we imply two things: the fact that He was God has not made Him into a man alien to us, a man so different from us that He has only the same shape and the same name while in reality He has nothing in common with us; on the other hand, we proclaim that being the true man means to be a revelation of man in his fulfilment, man as he is called to be, and that in Christ we have a vision—*concrete, real, historical*—of what we are called to become in our reality, in our historicity and in our becoming. So when we say that Christ is true man, we affirm that to be united with the Godhead does not annihilate or change the nature of man, and it is only in Him, because man is united in Him with the Godhead, that man is revealed in his full potentiality. Because man as a specimen of natural history is not man in the sense in which we believe man is truly human. Man becomes truly human only when he is united with God intimately, deeply, inseparably, so that the fullness of Godhead abides in the flesh. I am using terms which are applied to Christ in the Scriptures, but which I believe are applicable to man if we take, for instance, the words of St Peter in his Epistle that our vocation is to become partakers of the divine nature— God's participators and not just human beings related to a God who remains an outsider to us. But that implies a quite different vision of man, and it also implies something which I believe to be important, a quite different vision of the Church.

It is necessary to emphasise very strongly the profound difference between the atheist notion of the collective and the notion of the Church, in which we are members of a living body; likewise between the notion of the 'individual' and that of the 'person' which is the condition of man within the Church.

The collective position is that in which an ideological minority becomes a *de facto* majority, having the right to impose its will on each member of the society. In the Church there is nothing of the sort. Even the will and word of God have no authority in the sense of a law which is imposed. It is a voice which reveals to us the reality and truth of things. If we respond to it, we do so because we are sensitive to the truth of what is proclaimed to us and we reach out towards this reality, which is the only means we have of becoming fully free and fully ourselves. The will of God is not a law or an imprisonment. One of our Russian theologians of the 19th century, Khomyakov, tells us that the will of God is a malediction for the demon, it is the law for unregenerate man, and freedom for those who have attained salvation. In these terms, which are perfectly adequate to the theme, we see that it is not a question of a will imposed from outside, but of a will that appears external to us in the measure in which we ourselves are external to our vocation and to our human reality.

On the other hand, in the atheist world of the collectivity it is a will of iron that is imposed on its members: it pours scorn on the convictions and the most categorical imperatives of conscience, because the truth is expressed by the Party, or else by such and such a human group that considers itself to be in possession of the truth and of the right to define it according to needs and convention. In this view man is seen as an individual who has no supra-personal life, no life that transcends him and means that he lives in others and others in him; he forms part of a pattern, he is one of the constituent but replaceable elements.

We see the tragic working of this not only in the Russian Revolution but even in the story of the members of the Party in the time of the Stalinist purges. One can read the book *Into the Whirlwind* by Eugenie Ginsburg, who was a member of the Party before the Revolution, passionately devoted to her party, and who spent eighteen years in concentration camps simply because she refused to sign a list of statements of confession to crimes that she had never committed but which were useful at the moment to her party's line.

According to Marxist ideology, the individual is an interchangeable being; in contrast, the person is unique and irreplaceable: this is a profound difference that exists within and without the Church. I should like to indicate briefly the difference between these two terms by saying that an individual is the last term of fragmentation of mankind—races, nations, groups, families: it is not possible to divide further than the individual. If you endeavour to go further in your attempt at dissection, you will get a corpse and a soul: you will no longer be in the presence of the whole human being.

The person is altogether different. This can best be defined by the passage from the Book of Revelation in which we are told that in the Kingdom of God each of those who enter will receive a white stone with a name inscribed on it—a name known only to God and to the one who receives it. This name is not the nickname by which we are known in ordinary life—surname, Christian name—it is a name that contains, and defines all that we are and all that we are called to be. We can imagine it to be the mysterious word that God uttered in order to call us into being out of nothingness, out of the radical absence from which we were drawn by the will of God. This name, which defines us completely and is known only to God and the one who bears it, defines the unique, unprecedented and unparalleled relationship that each of us has with God. In this relationship persons are not opposable, individuals are indeed: we recognise them by contrasting traits of character, external features, psychological and social traits; we speak of their colour, stature, weight, nationality. Here the question does not concern those things: it is a question of something very profound and unique, such that it is not by contrast or opposition or comparison that we recognise the human person, but by the fact that *he is himself* and that no one has ever been or ever will be what he is, because if two persons could be identified with one another, they would be one. Thus we see clearly that the collective, which deals with individuals, and the Church, which is composed of members who are unique, irreplaceable and inimitable, are profoundly different realities.

Very often we think of the Church in sociological terms; it is a society of men gathered around a teaching, round a person, round certain functions, some of which are liturgical—worship—or acts of God—sacraments— but which always belong to a human society directed Godward. This is a poor and deficient vision of the Church. Looked at from this angle, the Church is nothing more than an object of historical study; it is not an object of faith, there is no invisible depth in that kind of vision of the Church. This presence of the invisible belongs to the Church because the first member of the Church is the Lord Jesus Christ, who from two aspects transcends the empirical, historical Church which we are, defined in the words, if you like, of St Ephraim of Syria, as not the assembly of the just, but the crowd of the sinners who repent and are seeking for eternal life. Christ transcends this empirical, historical, sociological group by the fact that as man in His very humanity, He is completely what we are, yet without our brokenness, without our separation from God, without our separation from one another. Sin means basically separatedness, brokenness—within us a sort of schizophrenia, outside among us the fragmentation which we define when we see one another, not as parts, members, limbs of one body, but as individuals contrasted with us.

But Christ also transcends the sociological reality of the Church in another way. Even while He was within history in the days of His flesh, He belonged at the same time to the fullness of eternity because He is God, not only in His Godhead but because His humanity itself transforms life —finite, precarious, transitory as we know it—into Life Eternal, stable and victorious.

The Church is also the place where the Holy Spirit has taken abode, indwelling each of us and making each of us a temple of the Divine Presence, and through the Holy Spirit we are united in one life, one reality, both physical and spiritual, with the Son of God, and we become, by participation, by adoption, the sons of the Father. The Church is an organism, both and equally human and divine, containing the fullness of God and the fullness of man, but also the frailty and brokenness and insufficiencies of man, and in that sense the Church is simultaneously already at home and still becoming—already at home in terms of relatedness to God by the way in which we are already grafted on God, and still becoming because we have not reached the fullness to which we are called. In that sense, the Church also participates in this curious historicity and transcendence of Christ Himself. Historical, yes, but bringing into history a dimension which is not to be imprisoned in time and space; the dimension of infinity, of eternity, of profundity, which things do not have apart from their participation in these qualities which are God Himself.

Now I want to turn to Christ, and to speak a little about his humanity. We read that He is truly man, and when we try to see what He has in common with us, we see that He was born, He lived, He died. When we think of the way in which He participates in our life, we see He is not only a partaker of the glories of mankind—rather of anything but its glories. He identifies Himself, not merely with those who are in glory, not merely with those who are just, righteous and saintly, not merely with those who are in no need of salvation or help—He identifies Himself with everyone. We must not forget that the rich and the wealthy and the powerful also have an eternal soul, an eternal destiny; we must remember that to preach the Gospel to the poor and the derelict is only half of our mission. I am afraid the Church has forgotten that, and for centuries has preached patience to the one, hardly ever preaching justice to the other.

But it still remains that Christ, in His acceptance of the human situation, has identified Himself with us, not only in our stability but also in our frailty and in our misery.—Yes, He hungered with us, He was born, rejected; there was no place for Him except in a manger outside the society of man. He was tired, He was abandoned, lonely, hated, despised, and so forth; that is also true. He accepted the company of people whose company others didn't want—the sinners, those who were despised; that is also true. But there is something more to the way in which He accepts solidarity with us, and something much more important. He accepts solidarity with us *in death*. One says, quite naturally: He chose to become a man, so He had to die. No, He hadn't, and this is just the point. This prevents people from understanding what is special about the death of Christ. If it is in terms of death, all those who are mortal die, and He did nothing that each of us will not have to do some day. If it is in terms of suffering, there are millions of people who have suffered infinitely more than He did on the cross. Two thieves were crucified at the same time as He, they also died a human death on the cross. If we think of the eleventh chapter of the Epistle to the Hebrews, we see that human suffering, human horror, even in terms of holiness, have surpassed all that we can imagine of the physical suffering of Christ. The tragedy of His death is not His ultimate participation in human tragedy and human destiny.

The *unique* human tragedy, the only one that counts, the one from which all others arise, is *mortality*, and this mortality is linked with sin, as separation from God. And it is here that the death of Christ and His solidarity with us contain something more frightful than we can imagine. A number of writers have pointed out the fact that death can be conceivable only through severance from the source of life. One cannot be, as it were, plugged into life eternal and die. St Maxim the Confessor underlines the fact that at the moment of His conception, at the moment of His birth, in His very humanity Christ had no participation in death, because His humanity was pervaded with the eternal life of His divinity. *He could not die.* It is not an allegory or a metaphor when in the Orthodox Church on

Thursday in Holy Week, we sing 'O Life Eternal, how can you die; O Light, how can you be quenched?'

He died on the cross, and His last words are the most tragic words of history. He, who is the Son of God, because He has accepted total, final, unreserved and unlimited solidarity with men in all their conditions, without participation in evil but accepting all its consequences; He, nailed on the cross, cries out the cry of forlorn humanity, 'My God, my God, why hast thou forsaken me?' People who are keen on exegesis explain to us that at that point He was repeating a verse of a prophetic psalm. If you have seen anyone die a violent death you cannot well imagine him at the last moment rehearsing a prayer he had been taught when he was a little boy! Besides, it is an error of vision—for it is prophecy that is turned towards its fulfilment, not Fulfilment that is supposed to recite words of prophecy. No, it was something real. When Christ said 'My God, my God why hast thou forsaken me?', He was crying out the words of a humanity that had lost God, and He was participating in that very thing which is the only real tragedy of humanity—all the rest is a consequence. The loss of God is death, is desolation, hunger, separation. All the tragedy of man is in one word, 'godlessness'. And He participates in our godlessness, not in the sense in which we reject God or do not know God, but in a more tragic way, in a way in which one can lose what is the dearest, the holiest, the most precious, the very heart of one's life and soul. His death is not only a simple acceptance of the human condition; it is conditioned by the ultimate experience of the human tragedy, which consists in losing God and dying because of this. Here we have something extremely important: Christ in His Incarnation accepted not only the limitations but the depth of our tragedy. According to the old saying, what Christ has not participated in remains outside the mystery of salvation. If Christ had not participated in our break with God, in our estrangement, in what a theologian calls a 'metaphysical swoon' which made Him lose sight of the presence of God. He would not have participated fully in our mortality, and our mortality would have been outside the mystery of the Redemption.

Thus we see how far divine love reaches in this solidarity with us: Christ accepts not only being like one of us, not only participating in everything except sin, but participating even in 'estrangement', in the fact of becoming a stranger, of withdrawing from the Father in order to participate in the unique tragedy of man: the loss of God—'atheism'.

The same idea is expressed in the Apostles' Creed, when we say, 'He descended into Hell.' Since Dante we have thought of a hell of torments: but the Hell spoken of in the Old Testament is not a hell of torments, it is something infinitely more horrid: it is Sheol, which is the place where every human soul is cut off, *the place where God is not*, because before Christ's Redemption there is a gulf between God and man which only the Redemption, the Christ-mystery can fill. He descends into Hell. Hell opens wide to seize a new prey in whom to press a final victory over God, without knowing Whom it is receiving. And into this Hell which receives a man God Himself enters. I believe there is a final touch here which explains what the psalmist foresees when he exclaims: 'Whither should I flee before Thy face? To Heaven? But that is Thy abode! To Hell? But Thou art there also!' Nothing in the condition of the created, nothing in the condition of man, except sin, is now outside the experience of Christ, outside the reality of Christ.

Everything is contained in Him, and there is not an atheist in the world who has known atheism, the loss of God, in the way Christ, the Son of Man, has who died on the Cross with that cry of ultimate anguish and agony. Here again we see the breadth of Divine Love and the depth of this acceptance by God of everything which is the human condition. 'Nothing human is alien to me,' said Tertullian. Perhaps he did not know how far this acceptance of the human condition went for God. He died. He died without sin. What death did he die? Ours, a borrowed death. Is not this our divine vocation, to be without sin and to die a borrowed death?

What I have said about Christ is said not about the God of Heaven who becomes man, but about the Man, Jesus, who had such faith in us, in all of us, that He became everything we are, including our godlessness and our death. He believed in us and was prepared to vindicate the greatness of man by showing us in His person that man is so great that when God unites Himself with him, man remains, in the full sense of the word—only instead of remaining small, he becomes what God has willed him to be.

I want now to talk about the fact that we do not only say that the Son of God became the Son of Man; we say, we proclaim, we believe, we see that God became flesh, the Word became flesh, and by flesh I indicate the fact that God became not only part of history or destiny, but of the material, visible, tangible reality of this world. Matter has found itself in the fact of the Incarnation, united with divinity. What I have said earlier about man holds here. The Incarnation reveals to us that man is so great that he can unite himself with God without ceasing to be man in the full sense of this word; that he is so vast that he contains the divine presence, that there is at the core of each of us what the Archbishop of Canterbury once called a God-shaped emptiness which nothing which is of the earth or of heaven or of the created can fill, but God alone. Here we see the greatness, not only of humanity, but of the material world revealed to us in the historical fact of the Incarnation. If God has taken flesh, it means that in an exemplary manner in the human flesh of the man called Jesus, all the matter of this world has been shown to be capable of such vastness, such depth, such greatness as to be united with the Godhead without ceasing to be itself, but becoming to a degree and in a way which surpasses imagination *itself* in the full sense of this word. So we discover that matter—which we usually treat in almost a sacrilegious way as inert, dead, alien to the great Promise to the creation—can become not only spirit-bearing, but God-bearing, pervaded with divinity. And we can see this in the way in which matter is revealed in the miracle of the Transfiguration. We do not see light divine shine around Christ, we see His very flesh aflame with divine light; we see His clothes become whiter than they can be made on earth; we can see that matter itself is pervaded, filled with the divine presence, and revealed in glory for however short a moment.

That is the background, the root of our belief and our faith in a realistic theology of the sacraments and a realistic vision of miracles. Miracles are usually thought of in a most primitive way by the least primitive people. People imagine that they are so sophisticated that they have outgrown the very notion of matter, forgetting that they eat every day, they multiply, they take baths; that they are the victims, fearful and careful, of every change of temperature. What I mean by a miracle is not something which strikes the imagination because it couldn't happen and yet does happen. The difference between a miracle and an act of magic is that an act of magic consists of an act of overpowering, of enslaving, of depriving someone or something—of freedom, of independence, of the capability to determine itself and to stand in its own right. A miracle is, on the contrary, an act of God which is mediated by the faith of man and the Divine Mercy that re-establishes a harmony, destroyed and broken. And at the root of it there is this very clear vision of the Old and the New Testaments, that all things created by God are created for eternity, with a destiny, capable of hearing God, of understanding God, of obeying God in a fulfilment which is both freedom and obedience.

That applies also to the sacraments in a peculiar way. In the sacraments we believe that the matter of this world is detached from the evil, sinful godless context in which it was betrayed by the faithlessness of men, brought back to God as an offering, received by God, made free, restored to its primeval freshness, and furthermore by an act divine, fulfilled and revealed as it should be and shall be. To take the central act of the Church, the blessing of the bread and the wine into the body and the blood of Christ—it ultimately means that we see here the matter of this world in the example of a small particle of it, of a drop of it, attain to that fulfilment which is the vocation of all things, that God should be all in all and that all things should be filled by the Divine Presence, indeed the integration of God in them.

That is the meaning of *Jesus*, which implies incarnation, history and the taking up of flesh by the living God; it implies a personal relationship which opens up our vision of men, of all things created; and it implies that the scientist, the physician, anyone who deals with the matter of this world, is a high priest or else he has betrayed his human vocation and in particular his Christian calling.

Among the ways in which we express our knowledge of things invisible and of God in particular, there are words which try to qualify God—either in His relatedness to us, as the Creator, or in His actions within our life of freedom—or else point to something which is at the very core of the problem. And there are three such words: one is *God*—God is a very fortunate word because it means nothing semantically. I don't mean to say that a philologist doesn't know where its roots begin; I mean that when you say 'God', the word itself hasn't got any content—it signifies someone or a notion, but it doesn't describe him. So that we can speak this word without prejudging anything. And there are two more words: *Jesus* and *Love*; the two ways in which we know God. In the word *Jesus*, we say who God is. God is this man who claims to be the Eternal One, Jesus, who is God and is man at the same time; to whom I can speak personally and who reveals to me therefore that God is a person because only a person can become one with a person, and reveal a person. I have already said all I wanted to say about the way in which Jesus of Nazareth, who belonged totally to history and at the same time transcends history completely in his Godhead, is involved and totally involved in our human destiny.

And on the other hand there is the word *Love*. *Love* which is not simply in Biblical terminology a feeling multiplied by infinity, but is the fullness of life that is beyond insecurity, has conquered death, and can give itself as an offering of life and death without fear. We read in the Scriptures that God is Love. We read also in the Scriptures, in a synthesis, bringing together things which are not expressed as a theological statement, that God is one in the Holy Trinity. The two things are identical. I want in a few words to say something about Love, then to try to show the relation of this notion of Love to the Holy Trinity—One God.

We usually think of love in terms of taking, of giving and of receiving; and this is right. But, first of all, giving and receiving is not quite what we understand by it. It must be something much deeper and purer, more refined than what we imagine we do when we give and when we receive. Very often to give is a way we have of asserting ourselves. We are rich and therefore we are secure, and the proof of our security is that we can give. We are proud and generous as a result and we revel in the sense of our generosity and greatness because it gives us the right to be proud. When we are at the receiving end at times, we can receive because we are greedy. But these two actions of giving and receiving must, to become Christian actions, be free from the evils I have indicated. You cannot receive with an open heart, with a sense of worshipful gratitude, with a sense of joy or fulfilment, of exhilarating openness unless you love the person who gives, and unless you know the gift is a sign of love and has nothing to do with pride and self-assertiveness. You cannot give in the right way if giving is not committing yourself to the last and is not an expression of service, of worship, and of tenderness. And this is one aspect of love.

But love is not only this. St Gregory of Nazianzis in the fourth century, speaking of God and trying to find the link between Love and the Trinity, makes an analysis of human love, because if we are using human words, human images, it is legitimate also to see connections on the human level. He says love that would be simply an arithmetical 'one', a monad, cannot be called love. It is self-love, self-adoration, narcissism. He turns to the love of

two and says that people 'imagine that the love of two, of
a couple, who know nothing any more except their love,
is fullness of love. Don't we see the passion, the total
commitment, the adoration, indeed, which results from
it?' And he says that this is a fallacy, because this love is
frail. However rich and however pure the giving and
receiving between these persons, this relationship is not
stable. The whole of literature, and unfortunately so
much of our lives, proves that the moment a third person
appears, we are either in comedy or in tragedy. It is either
Othello or Feydeau. It is either tragic and ends in death
and murder, or else it ends in the laughter of the on-
lookers. What happens is that this double link, this two-
way traffic of giving and receiving, breaks down if it is not
an open relationship, if it is a closed circuit that goes
round and round. When the third person appears, a tri-
angular relationship is established in which giving and
receiving can be pictured in the form of two arrows which
meet each other or are directed against each other. And a
new system of relationship is established—the newcomer
establishes a golden link of adulterous love with the one,
and a bloody link of hatred with the other; it is a triangle
of complex relationships, it is not an image of Love.

What Gregory of Nazianzis insists is that Love implies
a third quality—not only giving and receiving, but the
capacity for sacrifice. Now, the word sacrifice in our language means always losing something, being deprived of
something. But in Latin, in Greek, in Hebrew, in
Slavonic, in all the ancient languages, sacrifice comes from
sacred—it means to make something sacred, make something holy and not to lose it. Indeed, when you bring life
to God or a gift to God, it becomes His, it is no longer
yours in the greedy and possessive sense of the word. But
it becomes holy with the holiness of God, and we must

remember that when we speak of sacrifice, it is that which is the centre of gravity—not what we lose, but what happens when we bring the bread and the wine, the holy and perfect sacrifice. What happens is sanctification and not loss, because there is no loss when we bring something to God—we receive from God more than we could provide ourselves with. 'Seek the Kingdom of God,' says Christ, 'and all things will be given to you in addition,' not: 'taken away from you.' This is the principle of sacrifice, of santification, of the offering that gives and receives only as an act of love and not to gain a return.

The word which I would use is self-annihilation, the ability to accept not to be, no longer to exist in a situation because something else matters more. By this I mean the following: John the Baptist said about himself, 'I am the friend of the Bridegroom.' The bride is not his bride, neither is the bridegroom his bridegroom, but such is his love for both of them that he brings them together—he is their witness and their companion in the marriage feast; he brings them to the chamber where they will meet face to face alone in a fulfilled relationship of soul and body, and he remains outside lying across the door so that no one should disturb the mystery of this love. This act of self-annihilation is essential to Love, and if there is no such thing in our love with regard not only to one person but to all persons, all situations, all things, our love is still deficient.

This is very important for us to understand because in God we find the three things. We find the exulting joy of three Persons who love in giving perfectly and receiving perfectly, but who being a Trinitarian relationship, if I may put it in this form of speech, are not in the way of each other, in which each of them accepts every single moment not to exist for the two others to be face to face

—the miracle of total communion and oneness. Speaking of God we must consider things in the simultaneity of events and not in temporal succession. The three simultaneously give, the three simultaneously receive, the three simultaneously place themselves in such a situation that the others are alone with each other. But that means death because self-annihilation, sacrifice, means self-negating death and the Cross is inscribed in the mystery of the Holy Trinity.

We speak of the impassibility of God. So often the impassibility of God is understood as the inability of God to feel anything. The word doesn't mean that at all; it means simply that God is never acted upon, is never passive, is always supremely active. The Incarnation and the death upon the Cross, unless the Cross was inscribed in the very mystery of the Trinitarian life, would be an event introduced into God from the outside. In fact, on the contrary, it is the projection of one of the rich aspects of a complex mystery of Love into human history through the Incarnation and the death, because it is always there as the death of the one who accepts non-being in order that the others may be fulfilled. But then you will say, 'Is there any death within this mystery? Is it only death which we can expect from each other if we love in a more perfect way?'

Indeed not, because there is something else to it. There is a saying of Gabriel Marcel which I feel is one of the great statements of Christian thought in our time. He says 'To tell someone "I love you" is tantamount to telling him or her, "you shall never die".' We usually try to assert our existence, to be sure that we are, to conquer our insecurity, our doubt. We assert ourselves against people and things. We distinguish one another by contrasting qualities of size, colour, language and so on, that allow us to say, 'He is not me.' But this is the state of the individual, and the individual is a state of fragmentation.

This is not what is the object and subject of Love. It is the person that is our identity which makes us the same person from the baby to the old man, and from earth into heaven. This person cannot contrast himself or herself by opposition because it is *uniqueness* that is characteristic. But then, if you accept dying as an individual, dying as someone who tries to assert his being by not being the other, how can you survive? Only in the love of the other. And this is Trinitarian theology—the vision of three Persons whose love is such that they lay down their lives and are caught up into Eternal Life, into life that can no longer be taken away from them because they have given their lives and others have granted them eternity.

This is an anthropomorphic way of speaking of the Trinity, you will say. Yes it is, but the revelation of God is always in human terms because it is addressed to human beings; whatever can be revealed by God about Himself can be revealed only if there is a conformity between the object to whom it is revealed and the subject who reveals it. All that can be revealed must be capable of being put in human terms. What we forget and where we make our God extraordinarily small, and indeed not acceptable for many Christians and non-Christians, is that we imagine God is nothing but what can be revealed about him.

Between husband and wife there is a transcendence of two persons into something greater. A German writer has put it in the following way: 'In marriage two become one in such a way that it is one personality in two persons,' and beyond that there is all the mystery of God which is beyond communicating, which is beyond being shared with us. In that way then we will see that God is infinitely vaster than the model and image that we have, but all these models and images belong also to the mystery of revelation. A God like Him is, on all these levels, to us a revelation of transcendence and at the same time, of humanity. He is as great as man is, and we are as great as He is. He belongs to our becoming and our tragedy, totally, and we belong to the fullness of His glory, wholly by vocation, and yet, not in possession of it fully because we are still on the way.

If we think in that context about man and history and individual persons, about matter and science and technology, about the human soul and human art, then we can have a vision of the cosmos and of the God Who is within it and beyond it, that can inspire us to be creative, as creative as God, and, at the same time, to worship Him in amazement because we have been given this incredible freedom to be ourselves.

CHAPTER FOUR

HOLINESS

It is very important for the comprehension of holiness to understand that it has two poles: *God* and the *World*. Its source, its fulcrum and its content is God; but its point of impact, the place into which it is born, where it develops and also where it is expressed in terms of Christ's salvation, is the world, this ambiguous world which, on the one hand, was created by God and is the object of such love that the Father gave His only-begotten Son for its salvation, and on the other hand, has fallen into the slavery of evil.

God alone is holy. To say that God is holy is not to define Him as having holiness as an attribute, because we do not know this attribute. In saying 'God is holy', we do not define Him, because holiness itself is unknown to us: it becomes perceptible to us in proportion to our discovering God. For Israel—for the Old Testament—holiness was that which is God. Reverential fear was linked to this notion; likewise the sense of irremediable separation: God is transcendent in an absolute way, He is beyond everything. Even when God is known, He remains unknowable; even when He approaches, He remains infinitely far away; even when He speaks to us, He is still beyond all communication. To approach Him is a danger: He is the fire that consumes; one cannot see His face and remain alive. All these images show us the attitude of a people who were conscious of the holiness of God and who were aware of the Living God.

But the scandal of the New Testament, the impossible thing, is that the Inaccessible One has become accessible, the transcendent God has taken flesh and dwelt among us. The holiness which surpassed every human notion and was a separation reveals itself to be otherwise: the very holiness of God can become infinitely close without becoming any the less mysterious; it becomes accessible without our being able to possess it; it lays hold of us without destroying us. In this perspective we can understand the words of St Peter in his General Epistle, that we are called to become partakers of the divine nature. In Christ we see something which could be revealed by God but which could not even be dreamed of by man: the fullness of Divinity in human flesh. Here is the crux of holiness. It is accessible to us because of the fact of the Incarnation. This does not lessen the mystery of God: a purely transcendent God is easier to understand or imagine than the God of the Incarnation. And when we see the crèche of the Nativity in our imagination or in models or carvings and can take the Child-God in our hands, we are confronted with a greater mystery than that of the unapproachable God. How can we understand that the full depth of Infinity and Eternity lies here, hidden and at the same time revealed by a frail human body transparent to the presence of God?

All holiness is God's holiness in us: it is a holiness that is participation and, in a certain way, more than participation, because as we participate in what we can receive from God, we become a revelation of that which transcends us. Being a limited light, we reveal the Light. But we should also remember that in this life in which we are striving towards holiness, our spirituality should be defined in very objective and precise terms. When we read books on spirituality or engage in studying the subject, we see that spirituality, explicitly or implicitly, is repeatedly defined as an attitude, a state of soul, an inner condition, a type of interiority, and so on. In reality, if you look for the ultimate definition and try to discover the inner core of spirituality, you find that spirituality does not consist of the states of soul that are familiar to us, but that it is the presence and action of the Holy Spirit in us, by us, and through us in the world. It is not fundamentally a matter of the way in which we express it.

There is an absolute objectivity both to holiness and to the spirituality which is expressed in it. Spirituality is that of the Spirit; didn't St Paul tell us that it is the Holy Spirit who teaches us to say: 'Abba, Father'? Doesn't he mean that it is the Holy Spirit, God Himself, who shapes in us the knowledge of God? And, furthermore, there is no other holiness than that of God; it is as the Body of Christ that we can participate in holiness, in Christ and in the Holy Spirit.

If such is the case, a question of tremendous importance arises. In view of our search for holiness, in as much as it is situated, whether we like it or not, within the framework of the created world and the world of men, the tragic, complex world in which we live—if it is the presence of Christ Himself and the inspiration of the Spirit which the holiness of the Church should express in each of its members and in the totality of its body, *where is the limit of this love*? In other words, where is the limit of our sense of solidarity and responsibility? Is there a moment when we should detach ourselves and say: 'I leave you, go your way; if you repent, if you change, we will find one another again, but as you are, I can no longer go with you.' Or are there no limits, not only to God's condescension but also to this tremendous and passionate solidarity of God? Holy Scripture more than once places us in the presence of God's love in terms of 'Eros', that is, a love and attachment that is total and passionate, which embraces everything, leaving nothing outside.

I should like to draw your attention to a quotation which is certainly not scriptural and has no authority in itself, but which seems interesting to me. In the seventeenth century a Russian priest, a man of burning convictions, wrote his autobiography. He wanted to show how a man of faith can remain faithful to what he believes to be the truth in spite of the betrayal, or what he considered to be the betrayal of the visible Church. A prologue is attached to his *Vita*, written by himself. At one point in it he speaks of the Divine Council which preceded the creation of the world and suggests that in the light of what we know of God Incarnate, can we not say that one day the Father said to the Son: 'My Son, let us create a visible world and man.' And the Son replies: 'My Father, let it be according to Thy Will.' And the Father adds: 'My Son, you know that if I make it through you, there will come a time when man will play us false and in order to bring him back to us you will have to die?' And the Son replies: 'Let it be according to Thy Will, my Father!' And the world was created. This is not apocryphal, in as much as it makes no pretence of expressing a scriptural reality in other terms, but it expresses a profound inner reality: God in His divine Wisdom willed and called the world into being in full awareness of the consequences which this divine call, which made a free world appear out of nothing, would have for God Himself. This is a contest between God and the world, if we may say so, and the tragedy we so often complain about is more tragic for God than for the world!

Throughout the history of the Old and New Testaments we see how God afterwards takes full responsibility for His creative act. Step by step He upholds the prophets, declares His will, reveals the depth of His thought. Didn't Amos say that the prophet is he with whom God shares His thoughts? And He remains faithful when creation has become unfaithful—remember Hosea and the images he gives of the faithful husband of a woman who has deserted him. So underlying everything there is a unilateral act of God, but it is an act for which He takes total and final responsibility. This is important because if we are 'in God', we must share with Him; take our part of this divine responsibility. Our election to be the Church is not a paradisal privilege. It is basically an election to share the thought and heart of God, and to share Christ's work in the Incarnation and the economy of Salvation. I want here to insist on the intensity of this solidarity, simply turning your thought to those words of Christ, almost the last ones He uttered on the Cross: 'My God, my God, why hast Thou forsaken me?'

Here is the very core of holiness, because our holiness can be nothing else than participation in the holiness of God. And this is possible only through Christ, although the Old Testament was aware of a created holiness within the created world. Everything which God takes hold of and which becomes His own, such as the Ark, a person, a holy place, participates in a certain way in God's holiness and becomes an object of reverential fear. There is a holiness of Presence: the Temple. There is a holiness disquieting for the neighbouring peoples: the People of God, who are the place of the Presence. But this place of the Presence, which was like a living Temple did not participate in God's holiness in a personal way, in each of its members. It is only later, in the Church of the Living God, that the place of the Presence also becomes the place of a personal presence within and through each one: it is the Church, the Body of Christ, the Church which Christ is on the evening of His Resurrection, in the Holy Spirit who takes hold of the Church, and becomes its life; but it is also the Church each of whose members, on the day of Pentecost and through the centuries by a continuation of that mystery, become the temple of the Living God. And the Church is not only linked to Christ as His Body and to the Spirit, whose temple she becomes, but it is a Church in which each member in his particular uniqueness is linked to the Father through the only-begotten Son. 'Your life,' says St Paul, 'is hid in God with Christ.' Each of us is unique, irreplaceable and knows God in a way that no one else can share. This relationship of Christ with us, this bond between the One who alone is holy and His creatures, this presence of the personal eternity and personal infinity that God is, this real and living participation in a divine holiness is one of the essential characteristics of the Church. I believe that the Church is holy, not simply blessed and sanctified by gifts of grace, but holy with a depth and intensity which surpass all measure, holy with the holiness of God Who resides there, in the way in which a piece of wood glows with the fire that consumes it. And this holiness is a Presence in the Church. This is why the Church, in its position in relation to God, can acquire, possess and live this holiness only in Him.

On the other hand, just as God became man, just as His holiness was present in the flesh in our midst, living, acting and saving, so too now, through the mystery of the Incarnation, the Church participates in the eternity, in the holiness of God, and at the same time also in the salvation of the world. The holiness of the Church must find its place in the world in an act of crucified love, in an active and living presence. But essentially it is the holiness, the Presence of God, that we should manifest in the world. This is our vocation, this is what we are for. If we are not this, we are outside the mystery that we pretend to express and in which we pretend to have our part.

So if we as the Church are called to be a human presence of the kind that can be described in terms of sociology or history, we must nevertheless remember that this human presence is not the presence of an ordinary society. It is not only the place of the presence of God, it is also that of the presence of man, seen, conceived, lived in a unique way which is unknown to the world. And in our missionary work, in our enlargement of the limits of the holiness of the Church and of man in particular, if we lose sight of this, if we forget that it is God, and man in God, who is the object of holiness, we have lost sight of the essential. We can create organisations which are more or less useful—though they will certainly be replaced some day by more effective social organisations, because the possibilities of the total *socius* are greater than those of the particular society that we are—but we will never attain the goal which is offered to us, to be this revelation of the holiness of God, Who is winning and assimilating the world to Himself, making us participants in the divine nature and temples of the Holy Spirit, the really living Body of Christ, and making our life hidden in God with Jesus Christ.

Thus the element of holiness in the Church is found to be connected with a two-fold vision of man, but one that is different from that of the world. In this confrontation, this encounter between ourselves and the world outside, we must make our contribution to what man is—and we cannot accept the vision of a secular holiness which knows nothing of the depths of man, of his bond with God, and

which defines holiness in moral and pragmatic or practical
categories.

In the Church we have a two-fold vision of man: empirical man and the man revealed in Jesus Christ. There
is also the corollary fact that the Church is simultaneously
a society in history and, invisibly yet transparently, a
mystery. From the empirical point of view we are the
Church, all of us such as we are, not only such as we are
called to be, but as we are in the frailty of the individual
and in the insufficiency and implenitude of human becoming. From this point of view the Church can be defined in the terms used by St Ephraim the Syrian in the
sixth century: 'The Church is not the assembly of saints,
it is the mass of sinners who repent, who, sinners though
they are, have turned towards God and are oriented towards Him.' From this point of view it is true that the
Church is the object of history and of sociological studies,
because from that aspect it belongs to the world, for it
has not yet been liberated by holiness from the world's
grasp. The world is within it through us in so far as each
of us is not freed from the world, in the ascetic sense. This
pole of holiness which relates to the world therefore has
two aspects: a vision of the world as God willed it, as He
loves it, and at the same time an ascetic attitude which
requires us to disengage ourselves from the world and
free the world from the grip of Satan.

This second element, this battle which is our vocation,
is part and parcel of holiness. The Desert Fathers, the
ascetics of early times, did not flee from the world in the
sense in which modern man sometimes tries to escape its
grip in order to find a haven of security. They set out to
conquer the Enemy in battle. By the grace of God, in the
power of the Spirit, they were engaging in a combat. One
of the reasons why holiness seems so unrealistic and for-

bidding today and why the holiness of the Fathers and Heroes of the Spirit in the early days often seems so remote, is that we have lost this sense of combat. The conception of the Church as the advance guard of the Kingdom, as men and women who have committed even their weakness into God's hands, knowing with certainty that the very power of God is able to manifest itself in their weakness, the conception of the Church as the Body of Christ, whose life is not taken from it but which gives its life, is a rare thing among modern Christians. More often we see that as soon as a community or an individual is confronted with danger, he turns to the Lord and cries: 'Lord, help me, protect me, save me, deliver me!' Isn't this the picture which the Polish writer Sinkiewicz gave us years ago in *Quo Vadis?* in which St Peter leaves Rome at the moment of persecution and at the gates of the city meets Christ Who is on His way there. 'Where are you going, Lord?' he asks his Master. 'I am going back to Rome,' the Lord replies, 'to suffer and die there because you are leaving it.' Isn't this what we constantly expect of God? Isn't this our anguished, desperate appeal to the Lord as soon as life becomes dangerous: 'Deliver me, Lord!' When the psalmist spoke of this deliverance, his position was quite different from ours; he belonged to the Old Testament. We belong to the New Testament, we are the Body of Christ, the temple of the Holy Spirit. God has sent us into the world by His Son, just as He sent His Son into the world.

And so in this respect there is a crisis of holiness which does not date from our time, for it is contemporaneous with many Christian generations. But we must face it, because holiness is our absolute vocation, because contemplative holiness is not an escape, and because the activism of our time which tries to be independent of any contemplation and to become a value in itself, lacks the content of complete holiness which Christian holiness ought to have, for the content of holiness is God Himself.

It is necessary to define the position of the Church and that of the individual Christian in relation to the world. It seems to me that we have only two ways of doing this: on the one hand, we can try to see what holiness has been in history, and on the other hand, we can try to understand, in the person of Christ and in divine love, what the world is for God and what the solidarity of God is with regard to the world that He has created.

I believe that a careful study of the history of the saints will easily show us that throughout the ages holiness has been the expression of love. In the very brief and condensed history of my own Church—it is hardly a thousand years since we Russians became Christians—we can see something extremely important: the forms of saintliness have changed through the centuries (without disappearing once they have come into being), and these changes express through the years the way in which God, in the hearts of the faithful, has loved the world.

Scanning the history of the Russian Church—the one I know best—I see that at the beginning there is an act of faith: a man or a human group who believed, and who gave God to the surrounding people. St Vladimir, Prince of Kiev, believed. And because he believed passionately, radically, Christ entered into the history of his principality, and the social and human structures began to break up and be transformed. Yet he had no social purpose, no pious work in view: he simply could not live otherwise than he had learned from God Himself. It is only because this man believed in the Gospel message that the relations and internal structures in his principality changed. It is curious to note this change during a period when there was certainly no talk of social security or of a state responsible for its citizens! We see in the first place that this man, who had been a man of war and violence, a powerful and authoritarian tribal chief, ceased to make war, opened the prisons and proclaimed the forgiveness of Christ. We see that this man, whose personal life was by no means a model of holiness, changed overnight with a suddenness and finality which confronted his people with a choice: to follow the old vision or a new one. We see that in this little city of Kiev, which was no more than a market-town, the poor, the sick and the aged became the object of solicitude. All the poor who could still walk received their daily meal in the courtyards of the Prince's palace. For those who were too old, too weak, unable to move about, the Prince sent carts loaded with bread and sustenance through the city and neighbouring hamlets. Here we have a picture of a social transformation as great, comparatively speaking, as the greatest of our time. It implies a change of mental habit more amazing than the improvements that we make from day to day within one mentality already acquired and given to us.

This is the first picture: living, active love, the diaconate of Christ. Then, a little later, we have the witness of the martyr, a particular type of martyr. There is no doubt that the Russian Church, like all the others, has known martyrs for the faith: people who set out to preach the Gospel to tribes that were still pagans, perished for their message. Among them are two men who expressed a type of holiness that we would call 'social'. They were two princes, Boris and Gleb—and even a third, Igor—who chose to give up their power and principality and their very life rather than draw the sword. They allowed themselves to be killed rather than be defended and cause bloodshed. Here again is an example of holiness contemporaneous with an era of violence, one in which violence breaks out in new forms and in a new situation. Here again we see that the Gospel creates a situation of love, and that it is love alone which defines holiness in this situation.

After that there is a dark age: Russia is invaded and for three centuries falls under the Mongol yoke. At this time we find two types of holiness, that of bishops and that of princes, both of which express the same thing. Their holiness arises out of the fact that both are hard pressed, being the defenders, advocates and protectors of the people committed to their charge, and they give their life, their blood, for the people. At this moment all the other forms of holiness that have existed—monastic holiness and others—become sporadic. This is followed by a veritable epidemic of communal holiness: that of people who give their lives for their neighbour, truly taking responsibility for him according to the image of the Kings and Priests which the Old Testament gives us. They realise that sometimes, in so-called 'better' times, the heads of the Church, as well as those of the state, forget that they stand on the threshold of two worlds: the world of men and the world of God; the world of the unique, radiant Divine Will directed to the salvation and plenitude of all things, and the world of multiple, discordant, violent human will opposed to that of God,—and that their role is to unite the two and to give their life for this work. Once again we see that it is love that takes the lead. It was not a new invention in terms of holiness, it was not the search for a contemporary holiness: it was simply the response of the holiness inherent in the Church, of the love given by God to His Church, which had found a new form of expression. It was not the moment to withdraw into the forests or to choose other valid but different forms of holiness: it was the moment for giving one's life.

The Mongol yoke withdraws: we enter a period of national uncertainty, a period in which former suffering now changes to confidence. As long as this suffering was crushing the nation and destroying the very capacity to feel it, it was bearable. Now problems arise, internal ones which are not yet well expressed: God and suffering, the horror of a world which could be so frightful, and then the birth of hope and the search for a path for this hope. At this time we see giants of the spiritual life, one after the other, abandoning everything, the highest tasks as well as the humblest circumstances, and withdrawing into the forests of northern and central Russia to seek God there. These men leave everything because they have understood that in torment, disorder and purely earthly seeking they will not find the answer to the problems of their contemporaries. They leave everything to be with God. Their purpose is certainly not social at this time. They have to find their souls again, and with their soul, the soul of their nation, the soul of their people, the soul of their contemporaries. They are not in flight: they take up a life so arduous, so laborious that it would be ridiculous to consider it as an escape. The living conditions in a forest in northern Russia at this time, the hunger, cold, physical dangers from wild beasts, all these should make it easy for us to understand that it is not a soft and comfortable life that they are looking for. They seek only God, and they find God in the depths of their souls, which surrender to Him. They seek only Him, but at the same time their love becomes deeper and deeper, and they welcome all those who, one after the other, come in the same anguish, seeking the same haven of salvation. Monasteries grow up around them, this too by an act of love. A society of human solidarity and work begins to appear. I will give two examples that are diametrically opposed.

In northern Russia beyond the Volga in the fifteenth century one of the great saints of Russia, St Nil Sorski, settled with several companions in a desolate, swampy region. They lived in dreadful poverty, and in his *Rule* St Nil Sorski said that a monk must be so poor that he cannot even offer physical charity beyond a piece of bread. But he should love the pilgrim or the vagabond or the brigand who has fled or the heretic who has broken away from the Church—he should love him so much that he would be ready to give him all his spiritual experience, everything that his soul contained. Here is a man who chose to know only Christ, and Christ crucified, who gave up everything physically, and who could not give anything, for he possessed nothing but God alone, by Whom he was possessed. For one does not possess God: one is laid hold of by Him, filled with His breath and His presence.

The other man, his contemporary, lived in the region of Moscow and was an equally remarkable person. He founded a monastery in which about a thousand monks worked under a rule of incredible austerity. The monastery, in such a cold region, was never heated; the monks were not permitted to wear anything else but a hair shirt and a garment thrown over it. The offices lasted ten hours a day and the work in the fields or in the monastery for seven to eight hours. At times they groan and wail with indignation, saying, 'We are hungry, our granaries are full . . . and you do not let us eat; we are thirsty and we have water . . . and you do not let us drink.' Their holy and fierce superior answers: 'You do not work in order to be satisfied, you do not work in order to have a life of ease; you have no business to be warm, you have no business to be at rest. Look at the peasants round about, they are hungry, it is for them that we must work; they are cold, it is for them that we must cut wood; they have many orphans, it is for them that you set up this orphanage; they are ignorant, it is for them that you have this school; the old people have no place to go, it is for them that you must maintain this old people's home.' And these poor thousand monks, some of whom were doing their utmost to be holy, groaned and groaned . . . And nevertheless, under the strong hand of their Superior they lived a life which was love. There were moments when they rebelled, when the flesh weakened, but they had a conscience in their midst; it was St Joseph, who did not allow them to fall as low as they would have. To use more modern terminology, he is, if you like, a collective superego. He is there with his absolute demands.

Other monasteries of the same kind formed round him. Hunger, cold, ignorance, neglect of the aged, neglect of the young: all this became the object of active concern. And if you read the works and life of St Joseph, there is no doubt that there was nothing else but love, for he had no concern for anything else. He did not care about the consequences, nor did it matter what people thought of the folly of his ways. What he said was that these people were hungry and in need of help, and that we who have known Christ, who know who He is, must bring Him to them. And if it costs you your life, well, it costs you your life! If you read his writings, you will see few reassuring passages on the repose which the monks will have and a much greater number in which they are warned that if they do not toil hard, hell fire awaits them!

After this epoch we find ourselves in a period in which states begin to acquire a reality which we would now call secular. The principality of Moscow begins to grow in strength and size. It devours the neighbouring principalities by most unworthy means and asserts a new kind of ethic, a state law. At this moment the Christian conscience rises up in a very curious way. During this period, which was a time of renewal, when people were simply beginning to breathe again and also to attach themselves more and more to material goods—because they had begun to appear and because everyone was happy to be able to build a livable world at last—a group of men and women, several dozen, appeared successively and simultaneously, who were called 'God's fools' or 'fools for Christ'. On close inspection the folly in question can be interpreted in two different ways according to the various cases. There was the folly undertaken by people of luminous intelligence, burning hearts and iron will. But there was also, in certain cases, the holiness of those whose intelligence was disturbed but who, basically, had God at the heart of their interior life. They were people who denied all the social values: wealth and the impossibility of living without many of the material things so dear to man, the most basic human relations as well as the most demanding hierarchical relations. They were men who, in this icy Russia of the North, walked the streets with bare feet in winter, dressed only in a shirt, and proclaimed the fact that if you believe, you can live by the Word of God; *if you believe*, you can give up everything, whereas if you let yourself become involved in the new tendency to accept values that are only transitory, you are lost, you belong to the world of Satan!

Was it an exaggeration or a vision of truth? I believe there is a question of depth here. I have no wish to say that we should all go out and do the same and that none of the human values which the Christian world has formed in the course of centuries have any meaning. But

I believe that if we have a vocation, if we have the sense of eternity, the sense of the Presence—and if we know that God is living and active in our midst and in us—we should have a Gospel to proclaim. It would consist in saying: 'Yes, all of that has a value, but it is transitory, ephemeral and we must not attach our hearts to it. We must toil with our backs and our hands, but our heart must not be put into it, for our heart should belong only to God.'

Then a more complex situation enters into Russian history: social, political and religious life coalesce into one another in a way that is increasingly rich or increasingly impoverished, according to the moment. We find here all the types of Christian life that exist in the West, or in the Christian world taken as a whole, up to the moment when the Orthodox Church became the object of persecution in communist countries. At this moment the Church and the world become linked in a new way. If you think of the martyrs of the first centuries, you find that they are distinguished by certain characteristics. They were men, women and children who had discovered that God and Christ were the ultimate value for them, that in Him resided all the meaning of life. He was all in all to them. And it was out of personal loyalty that when His name was blasphemed, when His Person was put in question, they could only die for Him. On the other hand, in this relationship between Christ and those who believed in Him, a profound change was taking place in them: they would die to live forever. Recall the sixth chapter of the Epistle to the Romans. They died the death of Christ and lived again by His Resurrection, they were in possession of eternal life, and it was eternal life that powerfully strengthened and gave direction to their temporal life. For them to die was not to perish but to be released from a brief, evanescent life with the certainty of attaining the fullness, the plenitude of eternal life in God. To live was Christ, to die was gain, for living in the flesh also meant being separated from God.

We see, however, that it was only indirectly, so to speak, that the martyrs brought about conversions: it was admiration, it was awe, it was the revelation of God through them which made conversions, but their inten- tion was no more than to be witnesses of Christ, witnesses of the victory of God.

Since the Revolution, in this world of unremitting per- secutions which are sometimes terrible and sharp, some- times secret and hidden, a new mentality has developed. In this connection we can start with a thought that comes not from the Slav world but from the West. Jean Daniélou says that suffering is the meeting-point of good and evil. This is true, because evil is never something absolute, metaphysical and disincarnate: it always expresses itself in human persons, through human persons and to the detriment of human persons. Evil always slashes, plunges into human flesh or into the human soul. There is always a person-to-person relationship where there is suffering, hate, greed or cowardice. But the victory is decisive: evil falls into the hands of the good, so to speak, because the moment we become victims, we acquire a right which is properly divine, to forgive. And then, just as Christ said, 'Father, forgive them, for they know not what they do,' so can we in our turn say, as one of our bishops did before his death in the course of the Stalinist purges: 'There will come a day when the martyr will be able to stand before the throne of God in defence of his per- secutors and say, "Lord, I have forgiven in Thy Name and by Thy example: Thou hast no claim against them any more."'

This represents a new situation, a new mentality in the Church which is also one of the aspects of love, and is often too great for us because we are unwilling to attempt it even on a small scale. How often are we able to forgive completely the little sufferings that are imposed upon us, the small sorrows inflicted on us? But these men reveal a new upsurge of the love of God in human hearts, a new conquest by God. God manifests Himself once again, and the concept of the suffering Church and the personal martyr becomes at the same time a concept of the salvation of the other.

I hope that these examples will help you to grasp the fact that holiness is never in any way an individual act in the sense in which the word 'individual' signifies the last term of a fragmentation, the point beyond which one can no longer divide, and that holiness is always a situation and an act that imply not only the totality of the Church—since we are the living members of a body from which we cannot be separated and which cannot be separated from us—but also that we are members of the created world around us. Holiness is the love of God at work in a concrete, active, deliberate way, which applies itself with rigour and precision to situations that are always fresh and always contemporary with the eternal love of God and with the human presence of men, women and children who are possessed with this love and, living at a particular point in time, express it in a way that only they can choose, discover and put into practice.

As our holiness can only find its place in the created world where we are—I do not speak of society, because the anchorites and hermits are equally a part of the Church and have their part to play in the created world —it is only as far as we can see and hear, that we can act, or rather be, according to the will of God, so that our being is a creative and saving act, an act of holiness that would be our sanctification but is also a sanctification for the entire world. This is where the notion of wisdom has its special place. It is a wisdom different from human sagacity. We see it in the prophets and patriarchs and New Testament saints: their inner capacity for profound peace, for absolute stability, for gazing earnestly and patiently at the world in which they lived in order to discern in it the trace of the passage of God, the way He took, in order to follow that way, for it is He alone Who is the Way. And it is on this way that we can find and give the truth and the life.

This necessity of looking and seeing is expressed in a way which I find very beautiful in a narrative told by Nathaniel Hawthorne, relating a New World legend. In a village built on a high mountain cut by a stream and facing the little cluster of huts, very high up in the rock a face has been carved in time immemorial; it is the face of the god of these villagers. It is a face of transcendent beauty, expressing an ineffable peace and perfect harmony. And the villagers hand down from generation to generation a promise that there will come a day when this god will detach himself from the mountain and live among them. They admire this face, they are inspired by it—and they fall back again and again into the cares of their poor community life. However, one day a child was born in the village who, from the moment he was capable of seeing, perceiving and responding, of absorbing external impressions, as soon as he could crawl from the hut where he was born down to the edge of the stream, was struck by the beauty, serenity and majesty of this face. One could always find him sitting beside the stream doing nothing but looking.

The years pass, the baby becomes a little boy and later

a young man. A day comes when the inhabitants of the village, seeing him pass by, stop and exclaim, 'Our god is in our midst!' By thrusting his gaze deep into this face he had become inwardly conformed to the whole expression and spiritual content of those features; by gazing at it he had become imbued with it, he had allowed himself to be penetrated by the serenity, the grandeur, peace and love which radiated from that face of stone. And now his face had become that of the god whom he had venerated and quite simply gazed at.

I believe that there is something essential here in terms of holiness and also in terms of the place which human holiness can have within a complex pluralist society like that in which we live. If only we knew how to gaze with all the depth of our being at the face of Christ, that invisible face which we can see only by turning towards our own depths and which we see emerging from there, then those around us would receive the impact of a serenity, a deepening, a peace, a power both strong and gentle, and they would understand that there is holiness in the Church. And this holiness would have no need to make desperate efforts to manifest itself in order to make others believe that the Church is holy. Everyone would believe—which is so difficult to do when one looks at us!

CHAPTER FIVE

PRAYER

I should like now to speak about prayer in connection with what has been said so far about holiness. Prayer and holiness seem to me to be rooted in a twofold experience, not in two experiences but in a twofold, correlative one. On the one hand there is the amazement that we feel in the short—but real—moments when we perceive God, when we almost touch the hem of His garment. These moments of wonder are flashing instants of contemplation, and they leave us in a contemplative state, in deepening prayer, meditation and interiority which are on the border of profound contemplation and life in God. On the other hand, at the other pole of this twofold reality of prayer and holiness we find despair and compassion: despair such as we see, for instance, at the end of the tenth chapter of St Mark, the despair of blind Bartimaeus at the gate of Jericho, the despair of a man who has been blind and has suffered from it, who has fought for his sight for years and finally, crushed by misfortune, has settled into resignation. And then suddenly he hears that there is a man living in Galilee in Judaea who has the power to give sight to a man born blind, to cure every sickness, to heal every infirmity. And this man is passing his way. And this moment when the last hope is passing by is a moment of reawakening of all the feelings of despair that he bears within him as well as all the hope of which he is capable.

We can pray at moments when we become aware of our

blindness—and we can include in this term whatever makes us blind to God and to all that surrounds us—and when we sense that the One who can cure us is passing near. Prayer arises at moments when we become deeply aware of our separation and of the fact that our life is suspended over death, that nothingness is within us and lapping round us from all sides, ready to engulf us. And when we turn our gaze towards others, in place of that despair linked to an ultimate hope, which is the hope that Bartimaeus had, it is compassion which awakes in us, the capacity to suffer deeply, intensely, not the suffering of the other—for one can never suffer the suffering of another nor even understand another—but one can suffer from the fact that he is suffering, and in a mysterious way, beyond all experience, participate within this unity of the Body of Christ, in the common suffering which is his.

There is a link between the contemplation of God and an active, concrete prayer directed to the present and to the world in which we live. A Russian monk spent fifty years in his monastery without consenting to make profession, saying: 'I am unworthy, I don't yet know how to love . . .' And when he was asked: 'But what would you say a monk is, after all?' he answered: 'A monk is one who can weep for the whole world.' Here you see a man who had spent fifty years in a completely contemplative life, not oriented towards anything—in the last twenty years of his life he was bedridden because in the course of his work he had lost an arm, had lost a leg, had become blind—and nevertheless he refused the monastic profession because it seemed impossible for him to love and be a monk, that is, to be alone with God, not in a withdrawn solitude but in ardent and active solitude. Thus there is a bond which does not allow a separation between contemplation in prayer, the adoration of God, and action. But it is only to the extent to which our physical presence is the presence of God through us, the presence of Eternity in time through us, that we remain the Church while remaining engaged in action. If our activity in the world becomes a disengagement in relation to God, we fall back into the condition of a human society which has an ideology but no transcendent reality.

If we want to be active and contemplative at the same time, if we want to follow the line of holiness or communion with divine life, in a profound, intense, creative way while being at the same time in the midst of the world, whether in a cloistered order or actively engaged in life, we must learn a way of prayer that permits inner stability—not psychological stability (which we lack, but the problem is not in that, nor is the solution to be found on that level), but an inner stability which consists of standing immobile, face to face with the living God. We must attain to a prayer of presence, our presence with God and His Presence in the world through us.

I should like to say a few words about this aspect in order to be able to use it in what follows. Let me give you the story of the Wedding at Cana as an example of stability defined as a presence. You know the scene: a village wedding, poor and simple, with Christ, the Mother of God and His disciples. Long before hearts have been filled with joy, long before they are overflowing with that life, the human conditions for joy begin to run out. No doubt the lights are going dim, the bread has been eaten and the wine is dwindling. At this moment the Mother of God makes an act of presence; she makes the act of being there, fully and completely involved. As you will see, she is involved exactly in that twofold way which makes contemplation active and action contemplative. She turns to the Lord and says to Him: 'They have no more wine.'

What is Mary asking? Would she really like the Lord to perform an act of magic and multiply the wine until the guests have drunk so much that they fall asleep under the tables? Is this the joy that she wants for them? It is unthinkable. So there is something more in it; there is a premonition, a foreknowledge of the fact that if Christ gives them what the earth is now refusing, the gift will be one that is at the same time of the order of Eternal Life. Christ then turns to her and asks her a question: 'What have you and I in common? My hour has not yet come.' I know that there are pious translations which try to avoid a sentence that seems incomprehensible and difficult, that seems to be an insult to the Mother of God, and they do their best to translate this sentence too briefly to be perfectly clear semantically, by saying: 'What does it matter to you and me?' But 'What does it matter to us?' would be an atrocious thing for Christ to say. 'What is it to me that their joy is fading, what is it to me that this party isn't finished and doesn't reach its perfection? Haven't we who are sober had enough to eat?' Is that what He means? Certainly not, for 'My hour has not yet come' is a statement that pertains to Eternal Life and the coming of the Kingdom, and not simply to the magistery of a miracle-worker. 'What is there in common between you and me?' How are we to understand this sentence? St John Chrysostom comments on it in a way that seems to me more than strange: I believe he is in line with a certain modern psychology which always sees all the faults on the side of the parents. Here, according to him, not even the Mother of God has escaped this tendency of all mothers to believe that because they have brought a child into the world, they have imprescriptible rights over him. So there she is intruding, giving herself rights . . . and Christ puts her in her place. Saint though he is, I believe that in this case St

John Chrysostom has misunderstood the text. Other com-
mentaries seem to me more adequate. 'What have you
and I in common? Why is it you make this request? Is it
because you are my mother according to the flesh that you
feel you have rights over me?' (We are in line with St
John Chrysostom.) Or 'Has everything that you learned
from the angel, everything that you kept in your heart
and pondered in the course of your life, revealed to you
that "I am here", a Presence which makes this human
marriage unfold to the dimensions of the Wedding of the
Lamb? If you are speaking to me because you are my
mother according to the flesh, my hour has not yet come.'
He leaves the question hanging. The Mother of God does
not answer: 'Am I not your mother? Don't you know
how much faith I have in you?' She only answers him
with a gesture, but it is much more convincing than all
the words she could have uttered. She turns to the ser-
vants and says to them: 'Whatever He tells you to do, do
it.' She makes a total, integral, unlimited act of faith, the
faith on which the Annunciation was founded; the faith
that she bore witness to in being the mother of the Child-
God now comes to light in all its fullness. Because she
believed in a perfect way, she established at this instant,
in this village wedding, the Kingdom of God. For the
Kingdom of God is that in which we offer to God with a
pure heart a faith without blemish. There is an old saying of Israel: 'God is everywhere man permits Him to
enter.' The Mother of God, by this act of faith, established the conditions of the Kingdom and opened to God
the doors of this village wedding. So it turns out that the
hour of the Lord has come: it is the hour of the Kingdom,
where everything is in harmony with God because man
has believed. He blesses the water, and transforms it into
the wine of the Kingdom, into a revelation of something

greater, which makes this wedding that had begun as a human event unfold to the measure of the Kingdom of God.

You see what this presence and this holiness can be: the Presence of God, because one human person was present to God. When this takes its place in the world of the Church, we find ourselves in the presence of the People of God, which is the very place of the Presence. If we wish to pray within this situation, we must learn to pray in stability and silence: stability in the sense that we must find a way of praying while standing face to face in the immobility and deepening of silence, contemplation, wonder and anguish that are due to God's Presence. The reason we so often lose this Presence is that our very prayer, not only our life, keeps sliding and shifting. We start with one idea and turn towards another; we continually change our terms of reference. God remains Himself, but we offer Him prayer that is always changing, vacillating, reflecting all our external and internal fluctuations, and even conditioning them. If we say discursive prayers, we have to adjust our heart and spirit along a line that is often very complex and greatly lacking in sobriety in certain cases, whether the prayers are our own —often much too rich and elaborate—or those we find in the Christianity of the Middle Ages or Byzantine rhetoric.

So it is first of all a question of stability, of establishing ourselves before God. And this is by no means different from action or incompatible with it, because the sense of internal tension, the sense of haste and of movement are internal states that are not connected with the circumstances of our life. You have surely seen people who are old or infirm loaded with a suitcase and trying with all possible speed to catch a bus that is about to leave. They hurry desperately. And nevertheless, objectively, their movement is slow and heavy, their change of position minimal. You also know how easy it is for us sometimes when we are on holiday, when we are not striving towards any concrete goal, to feel wholly within ourselves, collected. One of the fifth century Fathers said that we must establish ourselves firmly inside our skin with nothing protruding outside. At the same time we are full of vivacity, we move fast and are capable of acting quickly. Why? Because we are not reaching after anything, the aim and content of our life in this situation is to be where we are now, whereas ordinarily, and nearly all the time, we live as if we were trying to catch a bus.

We have an erroneous notion of time. The amazing thing in life, said a seventeenth-century Russian philosopher, is that all the necessary things are simple and all the complicated things are useless. In fact, if we could only remember that time does not run away, that at a slow pace or at a gallop it rushes towards us, we should be much less fearful of losing it. Do you think that by going away from the hour of death as fast as possible you can prevent it from coming? Do you think that if you go on placidly, tranquilly reading, the hour of your deliverance will not come? In both cases it is time which is coming towards you, you have no need to run after it.

It is coming . . . and you will not escape it any more than it will escape you. Therefore we can establish ourselves quite peacefully where we are, knowing that if the time ahead has a meaning that is necessary for us, it is inevitably coming towards us at a sure and regular pace, sometimes much more quickly than we could run to meet it.

On the other hand, if we establish ourselves peacefully in the present, we are living in a world of realities, whereas if we hurry towards the future, we are moving towards a world of unreality. I think the importance of this is truly essential. We must know how to use time, the time within which we find all eternity, for eternity and time are incommensurable with one another. Eternity is not an indefinite length of time; eternity is not the presence of time without end. The difference between time and eternity is that time is a category of the created: it appears at the moment when something which did not exist before begins to be and to become, and it exists as long as the becoming continues. Eternity does not answer the question: 'What?' It answers the question 'Who?' Eternity is God, God who is always contemporaneous with each moment of time; He is always there, completely stable, unchanged and unchangeable because He already has in Himself, before the first thing was, all the richness necessary to meet all things and all situations. He does not need to change in order to be contemporaneous.

If we wish to learn this prayer of stability, then, we must first realise that God is in the time in which we are, He is in every instant, every 'twinkling of an eye', to use a formula of Romano Guardini's. If we want to draw upon this prayer of stability, we must learn this. We always know how to manage time when it is not a matter of God or of prayer; we do not know how when it concerns eternity! This remarkable, illogical situation is the constant experience of each one of us. Take, for example, what you do when you get on a train: you install yourself as comfortably as possible, you are at ease. From within this repose you look around you, you read, you speak, you think, I suppose you sometimes even pray . . . and you worry about nothing because you know that the train will arrive at the destination no matter what you do. There are some people who sometimes try to go from the last carriage to the first in order to be a little closer to their destination. Those who have a little more sense realise that two hundred *metres* out of fifteen hundred *kilometres* make no essential difference and that one can simply allow oneself a few hours' rest.

Why do we never do this in prayer? Isn't it remarkable that we should find this the most natural thing in the world when it is a matter of getting to another place, simply because we are sure of what is happening as far as the train is concerned—and yet there are so many possible hazards—and we are never sure of what is going to happen with God! It feels to us as though unless we are quick, mistrustful and active, He will escape us. In fact, in a certain way He does escape us. And that is not because we do not look for Him but because we look for Him everywhere where He is not. From this point of view Bonhoeffer is with us when he says that Christianity is a religion without religion, if we understand by the word 'religion' a system of methods that make it possible to catch God, to take Him captive, to get Him in a trap and keep Him there. Yes, in this case Christianity, and only Christianity, is a religion without religion, because God wanted to make Himself interior to our condition, and He wanted us to have no need to try to hold Him captive, Who became flesh in order to be with us. There is no need for us to try to use methods and techniques to make Him our prisoner. Not only is He in our midst, but He created this Church, which is not just a human society oriented towards God, but the place of His Presence, the mystery of the union with God, an organism which is simultaneously and equally human and divine, where the plenitude of God resides with the implenitude of men, leading little by little towards that accomplishment in which God will be all in all and the Church will encompass all things.

Hence it is a necessity for us to learn to master time in this way. For this there are techniques, techniques addressed to our restlessness, to our incapacity to believe in the Word of God Who has promised to be with us until the end of the ages. The first thing we could do is to compel ourselves to place ourselves in the Presence of God and to remain there a few moments without trying to escape—and without trying to give to this presence a discursive content, whether of emotions or of thoughts. If you sit down in a room and say to yourself: 'I am in the presence of God', you will see that at the end of a moment you will be wondering how to fill this presence with an activity that will suppress your restlessness. For the first few moments you will feel fine because you are tired and it is a rest to be sitting comfortably in an armchair, and the silence of your room gives you a feeling of quietude. All this is true. But if you have to go beyond this moment of natural rest, and you remain in the presence of God when you have already received from physical nature all that you can get from it, you will see that it is very difficult not to wonder: 'And now what shall I do? What should I say to God? How shall I address Him? He is silent. Is He there? How can I make a bridge between that mute absence and my restless presence?'

So one of the first things to understand is the importance of being and doing nothing in front of God. This does not seem very pious, and yet if you arrive at that repose which the mystical Greek Fathers of Mt Athos called 'Hesychia', a word that has given rise to a whole tradition, hesychasm, the tradition of the Jesus Prayer, a tradition of silent and contemplative prayer—if you reach that, then within that silence and immobility you will be able to do something.

But this immobility and silence, this presence with God must be learned. If you have learned it, you can try to do more difficult exercises: first, make your presence with God a little longer; second, learn to manage time, not when it is moving in a sluggish, meandering way, but at the moment when it is trying to rush like water from a burst pipe. It is simply a matter of saying at the moment when you are busy with something useful which must be done: 'I'll stop doing this, I'll keep still an instant and remain alone with God! All that I am doing can wait!' The Russians, who are not oppressively active people when they can avoid it, have a point of view which I think has spiritual value. One said to me: 'It is so wonderful: I can always be unhurried because if I do not die immediately I shall have time to do it, and if I die, it is useless for me to do it!'

Ask this question: does the salvation of the world truly depend on the letter that you are writing, the copper you are cleaning, the sentence full of wisdom that you are in the midst of pronouncing? Did the world not exist for millions of years before you said or did this or that? Will it not still live millions of years without your continuing to be a useful presence? So give it a chance now to enjoy your absence. Settle peacefully and say: 'Whatever happens, I will not budge.' Say to all those, visible and invisible, who come to disturb you: 'I am very sorry; I am here, but not for you!' This is what we are always doing. Suppose we are in conversation with someone and another person knocks on the door, you answer: 'I am sorry, I am busy.' If you are busy with God, you do not say: 'I am sorry, go away.' What logic, what common sense is there in this? It is not even a matter of contemplation, it is a matter of being polite!

Learn to remain in interior repose, peacefully and tranquilly, in spite of the telephone, in spite of someone's knocking at the door, in spite of the demon's saying to you: 'And you have forgotten this . . . you still have to get this done by such-and-such an hour . . . the brass is not shiny enough . . . if you added this sentence to your letter, you would be doing something worthy of the Fathers and Mothers of the Church.' But you answer him: 'If this comes from God, He will be quite able to remind me at an appropriate time, if it comes from you, I mistrust it . . .'

If you learn to stop time, to manage it in this way one, two, three, ten times a day, for longer and longer moments, you will come to the time when you can do it at any instant, no matter what your activity, no matter what the word or thought, whether in the liturgy or in everyday life. Thus you will be able to be interior to yourself, constantly face to face with God, asking Him unceasingly what you must do, what you must listen to. You will be fundamentally in the position of a monk or a nun: obedience, which consists of *ob-audire*, listening, listening with the intention of hearing—which is not always what we intend when we listen to our neighbour —of understanding what he says, of grasping what he wanted to say and of perceiving the depths from which this word came and what it is meant to make us discover.

I remember something my grandmother told me when I was a child. She was talking to me about the Greek war of independence against Turkey and she told the story of a soldier who, after the battle, in the dark night, called his lieutenant and cried: 'Lieutenant, lieutenant, I have taken a prisoner!'—'Bring him here,' answered the lieutenant.—'I can't, he is holding me so tight,' replied

the soldier. This seems absurd . . . and yet I have the
impression that very often it is the situation in which we
find ourselves with respect to the world, when we who are
prisoners of this world in a thousand ways—not so much
outwardly as inwardly—think that we can transform it,
and we are aware that we can only begin to do it when
we try to change our place and pull the world in our
direction instead of staying in the midst of it where it is
and imagining that our presence is enough to be a miracle
of transfiguration. There is something very important
here, I believe, for the way in which we will appraise
active holiness, in the world in which we are.

In the Gospel there is a commandment which seems to
me absolute, to disengage in order to engage ourselves in
a new way: we are called to be 'in the world' and not 'of
the world'. Not to be of the world is a radical disengagement. To be in the world is a total engagement, which
has the same radical sense of finality as the Incarnation,
which made of the Word of God, of the eternal Word, a
human Name and a Presence of God in the flesh for ever.
And there is that Gospel about rejecting those who are
closest to us at the same time as there is the Gospel call to
love the entire world with complete love, with sacrificial
charity, totally engaged. In this there is, if not a paradox,
at least an irreducible tension. The fact is that it is only
to the extent to which we are disengaged that we can
engage ourselves in a fruitful way. You know that if someone is drowning, you must jump in to rescue him but not
let yourself be seized, because otherwise you will both
drown . . . This is exactly the image of the Incarnation of
the Son of God and of the incarnate way in which we
must act in the world. We must be in the world without
letting ourselves be caught hold of, we must be free of its
grip. In terms of the theology of the Incarnation, this is

called 'without sin'. In terms of our life it would be an exaggeration to say so even in the sense of an intention or a hope. But one must be sufficiently disengaged not to be an integral part of the sin of the world, even if we do not succeed in freeing ourselves entirely from this imprisonment. We are called to disengage ourselves from the bonds which hold us prisoners, in order to give ourselves freely as Christ did: 'Nobody is taking my life from me, I give it freely.' Thus we shall be able to live and die, but in Christ's way, in the way of a Christian: to die freely and not have death forced upon us. Christ became fully man but without sin. He lived our life and He died our death, without, however, participating in the evil which limits our life and provokes our death. As for ourselves, we must be in the world and not of the world. It is only under those conditions that we become capable of loving, not with a passionate love that imprisons us and imprisons others, but with a love that is free with the freedom of the children of God.

In this disengagement-engagement there are two points to be noted. First, the necessity of disengaging oneself from oneself, getting free from oneself. We have an exaggerated tendency to think that we are prisoners of other people. In reality we are prisoners of ourselves, for if we could only release ourselves from the grip of our ego, other people would have no power over us. They have power over us only by reason of our covetous desires and our fears and hatreds. When we become capable of loving we begin to disengage ourselves from this prison which we are in. There is in fact a complete connection between 'loving' and 'dying'. To love means to disengage little by little from the exclusive interest that one has in oneself and to transfer that interest and that concern to someone else. The deeper our love is, and the more all-embracing it is and the more it is disengaged from the large categories of lust and fear, the more it frees itself from that aspect which C. S. Lewis so well describes as a diabolic love, which consists in the wish to devour and assimilate the loved one, making of him a total prisoner. Ultimately, the more this happens, and the more the egoistic self gets free, the freer we are. Subjectively speaking, perfect love corresponds to death, that is, to a disappearance of our self-assertion, our affirmation of ourself by contrasts and opposition in terms of aggression and rejection.

And it is only to the extent to which we become capable of loving that we become capable of seeing and perceiving. To see and perceive, whether it be God or the world around us, whether it be the individual neighbour or the more or less complex situations that include our neighbours, all this is possible only insofar as we love them and accept dying in order to be able to see, live and participate. We are surrounded by opacity, density: the world is not transparent to our gaze—and when I speak of the world I do not refer only to the cosmic world that surrounds us that we may sometimes grasp in the light of God, because it does not present a danger to us: we can consider it in its natural beauty and its harmony, without fear of being devoured or destroyed ourselves. But when we go back to our neighbour, whether in his individual aspect or in a wider collectivity as a social group, he becomes more and more opaque because all the judgements that we pass, all the reactions that we have are defined by a 'How?'. How does this person, this group, affect *my* security, *my* integrity? To what extent is there danger of or a possibility for expansion? When it is a possibility for expansion it is almost always in a very mitigated, and especially Christianly mitigated, form of aggression. We make progress with our neighbour, in our group. We feel secure because we have increasingly put our hand on something.

So we have a collection of opacities surrounding us. How are we to get through these opacities? For we go from clarity to opacity. A first meeting can reveal a person to us in the light. And then with the bad clairvoyance, or rather the progressive blindness given us by selfishness, coldness, calculation, the fact that we think of everything in terms of self, we begin to discern greater and greater opacities. It is only by an act of faith that we manage to say: 'Yes! this is a child of light!' We say it, but very often we do not see it. And this is why it is so often almost impossible for us—and when I say 'almost' it is a polite exaggeration—it is almost impossible for us to see the face of Christ in the faces round about us. This is important because it is fashionable now to look for God in one's neighbour. It is not a new fashion: the desert saints of the third and fourth centuries told us: 'If you have seen your neighbour, you have seen your God.' But they saw him, whereas we most often only say it! The fact is that in order to see the features of Christ on our neighbour's face, which is sometimes very difficult to read, we have to have in us the vision of Christ so as to be able to project it on them. Then we see, in the light of those divine features, that even in this portrait which sometimes has become so hideous, we can recapture the features of *His image*. I am not referring to passing ugliness, superficial evil, but to a profound evil more important than what one does, the evil that corrodes and causes the doer to lose the sense of the good—and the sense of what is luminous in himself—such people as one finds imprisoned everywhere, even in the Churches.

And so, at this moment, it is absolutely necessary to be able to recognise the light places through the opacities

and to recognise in the features of the portrait, retouched
from generation to generation by the whole heredity of
man, the conformity that we have with God. It is a question of recognising beyond the heavy materialism which
leaps to our eyes, that which transcends it. The world
around us, including our neighbour, to the extent that
we lack this clairvoyance, this insight into the depth,
appears to us as an opaque mass. This mass, these volumes
that surround us, with which we collide and almost never
meet—for meeting someone is looking at him face to
face, in depth—these opaque masses belong to a material
world to which we implicitly deny depth. The material
world has thickness: it has no interiority. I think I am
not being too complicated, in saying that if you are in the
presence of a glass sphere and you try to penetrate it with
your gaze, the farthest you can reach is its centre: it is the
ultimate point which cannot be transcended, there is no
other depth beyond. If you go further, you come out again
to the farthest surface. But all objects, even our neighbours, have only one density, one thickness, one heavy
presence, if we do not discover something more, that
which is revealed concerning them by Holy Scripture, in
which the psalm tells us: 'The heart of man is deep.' It is
not a matter of the heart of flesh nor of a measurable
depth, it is a matter of infinity, that is to say, of the fact
that the heart of man cannot be measured, for it opens
onto the depths of God.

This is why, in all our inquiries into prayer, it is an
interiority that we must seek, not the interiority of the
psychologists, of a depth psychology that belongs to the
realm of the created and at a certain point permits us to
touch bottom, like the final and ultimate point that is
the centre of a sphere. No, the depth we are concerned
with is correlative with the fact that we are a Will of God

become tangible and visible. At the heart of our reality is the creative Word of God. And the Word is the divine reality onto which we open in the depth. There is no use in looking for God round about. If we have not found Him within us, we shall never recognise Him in our neighbour, in historical events, in the heights.

If we have made the discovery of our neighbour in this way, if we have discovered that we have a depth that opens upon God, then we shall discover that very often our relationship with our neighbour can only be realised in silence. We all know in our everyday life those indescribable instants when at the most unexpected moment silence and peace descend upon us. When we are two who perceive this silence, when it envelops and lays hold of both of us, the words die on our lips and every gesture becomes a breaking of a relationship more important than anything one could express. If we let this silence penetrate us more and more deeply, there comes a moment when we can no longer express anything, when we feel that we are more and more close to a depth that we would never have known how to reach without the gift of God. When this silence has reached maturity, we shall discover that at the bottom of the silence there is a security and certainty that make us able to begin to speak. And then the words are sober: we search for them carefully before offering them; we utter them in a way that will not break this silence given by God.

There must always be, between God and us, a depth that we can reach—and I insist on this fact—that we should be able to reach. We should learn by the practice of the presence of God, by stopping time, by letting our being go deeper, to reach it almost at will, for it is our vocation to remain in the presence of the Lord. We should learn how to descend into ourselves when we are in the presence of our neighbour, whoever he is—not the pious one, the easy one, of whom we are ready to write in large letters: 'This is an image of God!' but the difficult neighbour, the unacceptable neighbour, the one who is an insult to all that we think of God and His Incarnation— we can then meet that neighbour in the place which no means of communication would enable us to reach, because we refrain from communicating on the level of words, gestures, external relations.

If we take our neighbour in this way, if we accept him in silence, we are making an initial act of essential importance: it is the act of justice—not an act of social justice, which is distributive, egalitarian—but a dangerous act of justice which consists, in the first place, of accepting our neighbour just as he is and giving him the right to be as he is, even if his way means our death and our destruction. It is an act of radical justice such as we see in God, who accepted fallen man instead of rejecting and destroying him; who accepted man in his downfall, knowing that the downfall of man meant the crucifixion of the Son of God. That is the act of Christian justice; it is there that justice begins, and not when we distribute spiritual or material wealth equally or selectively. It is the moment when we allow the other person to be *himself*, whatever the consequences. It is only at this price that we can look and see in the features of the other person a living and glorifying projection of the face of the Lord.

This implies something I have already spoken of: solidarity, such as we see in Christ. This solidarity with fallen man, man in his final agony, in his radical godlessness, or rather his relative godlessness—for only Christ's is radical —this enables us to take up our responsibility. But here I must point out that Christian responsibility and solidarity have a quality that makes them unacceptable and impossible on a certain level, because they embrace both parties in conflict. A Christian can, in fact, support one human group against another, but he cannot undo his solidarity with the other in favour of the first. In a conflict, whether it be armed, social, economic or psychological, the Christian should be present at the point of rupture and accept in a total way the responsibility for both sides.

I shall first give you an example in terms of canon law, from Church history. St Basil established a canonical rule which has never been applied—like so many canonical rules—which says that in case of armed conflict the Christian is called upon to take part in it, because 'if he had been a Christian worthy of the name, he would have been able to convert those around him to mutual love, and there would have been no armed conflict. But as it is he who bears the responsibility for the bloodshed, he should take part in this conflict. However, all the time the conflict is going on and for three years afterwards he must be excommunicated.' Here is a situation that is clear, precise, perfectly tenable theologically and of very great interest, which has never been applied because it implies at the same time the radical sense of bipolar solidarity and responsibility which is essentially identical to the Incarnation.

I cannot give you recipes, I can only indicate *three elements* as a conclusion to these considerations.

Interior contemplation, which is not a form of life but a position in regard to God, a standing before Him in a deepened silence; the double and reciprocal presence of God with man and man with God.

Prayer, in its active, human aspect, in its tension towards God, with the resulting inward state of orientation towards God and being present to God, and, lastly, its

final state which is a position in the world where we are:
the prayer of the world to God, the articulation of the cry
of the entire world to the living God. And this is obviously
an ascetic exercise to the extent to which we are under
our human vocation.

Finally, there is *action*, but as I said before, this action
must be an act of God, by our instrumentality. Let us first
learn to listen, hear, see and understand God, the world
and our neighbour. And then to act not solely according
to human wisdom but, above all, primarily on the basis
of the divine wisdom which is revealed to us in Scripture,
in life and in the sacraments—for the early Church
strongly emphasised that these form the gateway to the
knowledge of God and to action in the name of God. And
if in all honesty we try to live in God and to live His
presence in the world, I believe that in every situation
God will teach us how to do His will: the ways may be
different, opposed, incompatible . . . For if you read the
Old or New Testament, you will see that there are no
rules, no precepts—still less, recipes. There are divine
responses which may be mutually contradictory, because
when God confronts this fragment of time that asks Him
a question, He faces each situation with the whole of
Eternity.

CHAPTER SIX

INTERCESSION

The act of intercession is a prayer that is itself an act, and an act that is a prayer. Thus the action appears to us as a lived faith, something in which prayer becomes life. And if prayer and life are not the two faces of one and the same reality, one coin, neither one has authenticity. Christians spend their time interceding, and at times I listen to these intercessions with fear because to me intercession means an involvement that may spell death; and I am frightened when I hear a congregation of people intercede for one need after the other, piling up on their shoulders all the needs of the world just for the time that Evensong lasts. After that they put it upon God's shoulders, and they go out elated by a new emotion.

About ten years ago I came back from India. I was asked in London to speak at a rather big meeting about hunger. I spoke about what I had seen and what had wounded me very deeply with all the passion I am capable of. For a while the people sat and listened. Then when we came out I stood at the west door shaking hands, and a lady came up to me and said 'Thank you for the entertaining evening.' That is intercession very often with us. We have spied a need, we have become aware of a tragedy, and then from the security of our living, we turn to God, and say 'O Lord, haven't you noticed that? What are you doing about it? And this? And that? Aren't you forgetful of your duties to mankind?' This is not intercession. No, intercession is a complete engagement which makes us simultaneously engaged and disengaged from two sides, in solidarity with one side as well as with the other and, because of this, rejected by one as well as by the other. The Incarnate Word was killed by men because He was God; He was consigned to the cross because He was a man. He died a borrowed death which is a man's death. He was not accepted, because His witness was one that favoured God, from whom the people of Israel had already turned away. 'We want to be like all the nations!' they had said to Samuel when they asked for a king, and God answered Samuel: 'It is not you, it is I Whom they have rejected!' And the final rejection comes in these words of the people before Pilate: 'We have no other king but Caesar!'

Amos said that a prophet is one with whom God shares His thoughts and who not only receives the thoughts of God but, like a true prophet, proclaims them, lives them, witnesses to them, becomes an act of God. And it is to this that we are called in the Church, to be an act of God in the midst of the world. This is the special activity of the Church, which means that in all domains, political, social, economic, educational, the Christian's role has a peculiarity that makes it different from all the other functions in the world: it is an act of God and as such it can be in harmony with everything that goes on. One of the Christian obligations is precisely that of being not only the leaven in the dough but also the sword that divides the darkness from the light, truth from error, death from life, God from Satan, of being the stumbling-block, the scandal, the constant provocation, the constant affirmation that we are not seeking the kingdom of the Beast, that we do not accept a harmony based on apostasy, that we do not want a justice that is a denial of Divine Justice, a truth that is a refusal of the Personal Truth: 'I am the Truth!' and so on.

We are called to be that divine act by which God reveals Himself to the world, and, as such, our destiny can only be that of Christ. Yes, Christ did say to us: 'You will do greater works than I.' And it is true. In His power and that of the Spirit we are called to complete a work in which His action was decisive but not final.

We must be a witness to the world of the Presence, of the transcendence, of the fact that the Eternal has become immanent and is in our midst: God is in us and through us, God Who has no common measure with man, the divine mystery. At the same time this God reveals Himself in an incredible way which man could not invent, in Christ, who appears to us defenceless, vulnerable, abandoned to the discordant wills of men, surrounded by hate, rejected, Who dies because of this and whose victory is in His humiliation.

I believe that what I have said can be referred back to the image that Christ gave us when He said: 'I consecrate myself, I sacrifice myself for them.' I don't know which of the terms should be used, because the Greek word is too rich to be translated by only one of them. It concerns a prime act of consecration: it belongs to God without limitation. *It is God*, and not only that but in its very humanity it has only one will, a life with God, and this is a free act in which the two wills find themselves united in a perfect way, in which the two natures are inseparable, in which the Word of God listens in on the will of God and watches in the depth what the Father is doing, then continues to act and work in the world, to accomplish now what the Father wills in the mystery of divine thought.

He sacrifices Himself. To sacrifice oneself now means

to shed one's blood or to impose limitations on oneself in favour of someone—this is the way we are always sacrificing ourselves, doing a very little bit for our neighbour—but 'to sacrifice oneself' means 'to make oneself sacred, to consecrate oneself', and also to offer oneself or be given in sacrifice. Did not Christ say: 'Nobody is taking my life, I give it.' He gives Himself up, He dies.

What is our attitude in such a situation? These images which I have tried to give should permit us to feel our way, in the oneness of the ever contemporaneous Presence of God, into the multiplicity of ways in which this total Presence brings itself to bear, expresses itself, integrates itself into the variety of situations. But then our role also consists in being perfectly obedient, not in the sense of mechanical obedience, which would mean hearing orders and carrying them out, but in the sense of an obedience in depth which wants to listen with vigilance, tension, alert vitality, in order to hear and express what it perceives.

And this can be harmonious with what the world is seeking, because the Holy Spirit is not at work solely in the Church but everywhere, with a power and a force that are sometimes impressive. It is God who judges the Church at this moment by all that goes on around it, by the persecution, by the protests, by the atheism, by the rejection of the caricature of God which we offer for man's worship. And we most certainly must learn to assume our responsibility for the sins of the past, and not to bewail ourselves as we recognise them but to see in them the judgement of God as we endeavour to release that which is the Eternal Truth of God in the present situation.

I should like to talk now of the situation of being a Christian in the world; and I should like to preface my remarks by saying that we have a tendency to exaggerate the meaning which we attach to the expression 'the contemporary world'. The world is always contemporary to someone: at every moment it will be contemporary to a generation of people, and there are general rules that are human and historical which I believe can serve as a basis for our judgement and action. Another thing which I should like to underline is the fact that God is always contemporary. This we very often forget, trying by all sorts of theological efforts to make Him contemporary with us, when He is perfectly contemporary and needs no change to be Himself and to be up to date.

I would like to single out a certain number of features in the person of St John the Baptist which I feel could teach us something about our situation, and what we should do, and what disposition of mind we should be in. John the Baptist was the forerunner of Christ. He was the one who came before Him to make the pathway smooth, to make the crooked way straight. I believe this is exactly what all of us are called to do now with regard to other people, to make it smooth for them to find their way, and to help them to find a way which is straight, to the Lord.

First of all, when you open St Mark's Gospel you find that he is defined as a voice that shouts in the wilderness. He is not even defined as a prophet or a messenger of God. He is so identified with the message, he has become so much at one with God's own word which he has to proclaim and to bring to people, that one can no longer see him behind the message, hear the tone of his voice behind the thundering witness of God's own Spirit speaking through him.

This is one thing which we should learn. Too often when we bring a message, people can perceive us and a message which, perhaps, comes through us, because we

are not sufficiently identified with what we have to say. In
order to be identified we must so read the Gospel, make it
so much ourselves, and ourselves so much the Gospel, that
when we speak from within it, in its name, it should be
simply—whatever words we use and I am not speaking of
quotations—it should be simply the Gospel that speaks
and we should be like a voice—God's voice. The second
thing is that to attain to that state in which he could
speak and not be noticed, in which all that people could
perceive of him was a man who had been completely
transformed into a message, into a vision, into a pro-
clamation, meant he was a man who accepted the laying
aside of all that was selfish, grasping, all that was delight-
ing selfishly in whatever he wanted to have. He had a
pure heart, a clear mind, an unwavering will, a trained
body, a complete mastery of self, so that when the message
came, fear would not defeat him and make him silent;
promises would not beguile him and keep him quiet, nor
could the heaviness of the flesh, of the mind, of the heart,
overcome the lightness and the lightening power of the
Spirit. This is something that is also our task.

I do not speak now of the forms of asceticism or the way
in which one does it, but we must learn to be free, and to
be free, we must acquire mastery over ourselves. This is
terribly important, and to achieve that, we must learn to
look and understand, but not only to look at people and
situations—look at God and learn and hear. Obedience is
vital. To obey the will of God requires a training. The
will of God is madness, the will of God is paradoxical.
You cannot adhere to the will of God for good reasons.
More often what He asks is an act of folly which we would
not otherwise dare to commit. Remember Abraham: God
promised him a son, and a son was born. He promised
that the son would be the beginning of a generation of

people more numerous than the sands of the shores; and Abraham believed Him. And then God commanded him to take his son and to bring him, a blood offering, to Him, and Abraham did it. He did not tell God, 'That contradicts your previous command; this is contrary to your promise.' He trusted the Lord and did what the Lord said, leaving the Lord to fulfil His promises the way He knows.

This happens to us also. We are called to act day after day, moment after moment, according to the will of God revealed within that moment when the difference between Christian action and just action resides in the fact that action must be planned, action must not contradict action. There are no returns and moves backwards and sideways; it must be a straight course. If we want to act within the will of God, we must be like Christ who listens and proclaims the word, who gazes attentively at God Who is at work, and when He has seen, performs the action which is implied in the willing, in the thinking, in the rich creative imaginings of God. This we must learn, but to do this, we must learn to master ourselves and become capable of acting not only when we agree, not only when we understand, but when we disagree somewhere within the old Adam in us, or when we cannot understand but say 'I trust you, I will act with folly.'

The forerunner has another quality. Remember what he said: 'I must decrease in order that you should increase.' Our role is to cut straight ways; our role is to make rough ways smooth. But when we have done this, we must step aside, and allow the Lord of life, He for whom we are preparing the way, to come like a king, or with the humility of Christ in the simplicity of His entry into Jerusalem. And we must be forgotten because as long as we loom large, people will not see Christ. There is a way in which our absence is as necessary to the glory and action of God as our presence is at another moment.

Remember the other way in which the forerunner is defined. When speaking about himself he says that he is the friend of the bridegroom—the one who so loves the bride and the bridegroom that he brings them together, so loves them that he is the protector of their love, of their intimacy, of their peace, of their meeting, and whose vocation is to bring together bride and bridegroom—the living God and the living soul, and then stand guard to protect this meeting against any intrusion, but not to be party in this meeting, to be outside; that is his particular form of love and service.

At the same time, we must be prepared also to face, in the name of the bride and groom whom we serve, in the name of this mystery of love, the coming of the kingdom; the conquest by God of all that is death, evil, sin, separation, meanness which is too small for the measure and the stature of man. We must be prepared to speak to man the truth, God's own truth, not our own. Remember the way in which the forerunner spoke to Herod, the way in which he spoke to the multitudes. To do this we must have authority, and authority is not gained either by rank or by social standing. Authority is gained by this fusion between our own will and God's own will; our own word and God's own word, our own life and God's own life; then we can speak, and then our words, however hard, sharp, and deep they go, will also be words of love, because God's word is always the word that gives truth and light, love and life.

And then we must be prepared not to see the results of what we have done. The forerunner died before he had seen Christ. Coming to the end of his mission and fulfilling the promises of his vocation, he died. He died of his message, he died for the truth of God, he died because he had become identified with the message and because he was a friend of the bridegroom that had to decrease so that the bridegroom should have all the field. We must be prepared for that. In every case, with regard to every soul, to every group, to every event, to every situation, there is this time for the forerunner and there is the time for him to decrease and die out—perhaps not physically, but in the memory of people, in their hearts, in their relationships. We must be prepared never to be remembered because what has been sown by the word is so rich, so overwhelming, that the forerunner, the one that has prepared the way, the one that has ploughed, the one that has sown, can be forgotten. This is joy. It is joy to see Christ, the Lord, grow to His full stature, to occupy His real position, to be the king and the lord and the master and the brother and the saviour and the joy and the freedom of those to whom we have come and said 'He is coming, open yourself to Him.' This is what the scriptures call repentence or conversion.

The next point I wish to take up is one which, I think, is very important for the way in which we evaluate the world and our situation in the world: it is the notion of the *solidarity of God with the world*. I purposely use the word 'solidarity', which is neither theological nor pious, in order to avoid using a word, whatever it might be, that would put us right into an old rut where we could resolve without effort an extremely sharp and important problem. The measure of God's solidarity with us is the act of intercession by Christ which is the Incarnation. Intercession is a Latin word which means to take a step that brings you to the centre of the conflict, and in the image of Christ, in the person of Christ, we see that intercession means taking a step which is definitive—once and for all

He becomes man, not just for a while. And he doesn't come as a pleading advocate or a go-between equally indifferent to either side, who will go and find terms of compromise between the one and the other. He takes his stand in total, final solidarity between Man and God; turning to God, He is man and stands condemned; turning to men He is God and stands rejected. He must die. And His solidarity doesn't extend simply to the sweet selected few who will recognise Him or believe in Him. No, His solidarity extends to everyone. He is not God for the good versus the bad, the believers versus the unbelievers, a creed or colour or a nation or a social group. He has made Himself solid with everyone.

We discovered as exiled Russians in the early days of emigration when we had lost everything, when there was nothing left standing for us, when we were unwanted, rejected, despised, helpless, vulnerable to the utmost, we discovered we had also lost the God of the great cathedrals, the God of the beautifully constructed ceremonials. Where did we stand? When we looked at ourselves, we discovered that we had lost faith in ourselves, and very often self-respect. And then we discovered our God in a new way. We discovered that in Christ God had revealed Himself as vulnerable, as helpless, as contemptible, as overcome and vanquished, as trodden underfoot, as rejected, and we discovered that we had a God who was not ashamed of us, because He had made Himself solid with what we were, in our misery, in our deprivation, in our rejection, and also that we had no reason to be ashamed of a God who knew how to love to the extent that He was prepared to become one of us, and to show by doing this that His faith in us was unshaken and that His respect for human dignity was whole and untouched.

To bring into relief the place where Christ stands interceding for us and where we must stand also, I shall take as a starting point two stories of the Gospel which are too well known for me to describe them in detail—the stories of two storms on the Lake of Galilee. The scheme of these two stories is practically identical. The disciples leave the shore, they are caught up in a storm and they are confronted with the unexpected in the person of their Lord and their God, Jesus Christ. In the first story the disciples left the shore, then they were caught up in the storm alone in their boat. Christ had remained behind, dismissing the crowds after the miracle of the multiplication of the loaves and fishes. Their only protection against the storm was the frail shell of their boat. They fought with all their energy, with all their skill, with all their courage, yet death was enveloping them on every side, pressing hard, trying to break through their precarious security. At a certain moment they saw, right in the middle of the storm, walking on the seas, blown by the wind, Christ Himself. They looked and saw and they cried out in fear because they knew it could not be Christ, they knew it was a ghost. Why? Because they knew that God, their God, their Master, their Teacher, stood for harmony, for peace, for salvation, for life, and there He was right in the middle of the storm which spelt death, disharmony and horror. It *could not* be God, because God's presence could not be in harmony with what was going on.

This is the reaction we have so often, and we react as wrongly as the disciples when dramatic events occur in our lives. Whether it is history at large—wars and earthquakes—whether it is the small history in which we are involved—our own lives, our own families, our own religion, colour, group—if the presence of God is felt and is not accompanied by immediate harmony, by the coming of peace, by salvation, by the relief of pain and by the relief of anguish, we cry out that it is a ghost. He cannot be there. We forget that God is the Lord of the storm just as he is the Lord of the stillness, the serenity and the harmony of things.

I will leave this story at this point and take the next one, and come back to both. In this one we read that Christ has left the shore with His disciples. He is asleep in the prow of the boat; resting comfortably, His head on a cushion. A storm springs up, death is abroad, fear enters and conquers the hearts of the disciples. They fight again within the precarious protection of the shell of the boat, and they feel that they are being defeated. Then they turn towards Him who is their salvation, or should be; and they see Him completely indifferent, asleep, at rest, and—to add insult to injury—He is not only asleep but He has made himself comfortable with His head on a cushion.

This is what we accuse God of all the time. We never stop accusing Him of that. We are fighting against death: anguish disrupts our lives; fear makes them unbearable; death is abroad, suffering is killing us, and God is not only there, indifferent, but in perfect comfort because He is beyond reach of these things. Are we fair and are we right? I will try to answer this question a little later. Let us go back to more features of the story.

In the first story, having cried out in their terror, the disciples hear the Lord say 'Fear not, it is I.' They hear a voice which is strangely like the familiar and loved voice of their master. And Peter acting before he thinks, says, 'If it is you, tell me to walk on the sea and join you.' And then, because Christ says 'Yes, it is I, come,' Peter all of a sudden—because he has recognised Him who is life, who is meaning, who is harmony, in Himself—abandons the frail protection of their boat, and begins to walk on the water. And as long as he looks at Christ, and as long as his only desire is to be with Him, to be at that point where God stands in the storm, he can walk. But suddenly he remembers himself. He remembers that he is a man of flesh and blood, that he has gravity and weight, that he has never walked on the sea, never withstood the raging waves, that he will drown; and the moment he turns his gaze, his interest, his concern on himself, he indeed begins to drown because he is still in that part of the storm where death is abroad.

In the second story, the disciples feel defeated—death is there, they have no strength, no hope, no peace left. Turmoil has overcome them completely; they turn to Him, they awake Him, perhaps even roughly, for their words are harsh. 'For all you care, we are dead.' This is the translation which Moffat gives of that passage. 'For all you care, we are dead.' They don't turn to Him saying, 'You are the Lord, a word of yours will be sufficient for us to be saved.' No, they recognise defeat, they accept the ruthlessness and indifference of God, they have no trust in Him. What they want of this God become man who proves incapable of being a help and a salvation, if He can do nothing better, is to be in anguish, in despair, together with them and to die with them—not be drowned unaware, all unwitting of the oncoming defeat of life by death. And Christ turns away from them, brushes them away saying 'How long shall I be with you, men of little faith?' Then, turning to the storm, He commands the seas to be still and the wind to cease, projecting as it were, His own serenity, His own peace, His own stillness, His own harmony, on all things around Him.

In the case of Peter, as well as in the case of the other apostles, they had allowed the storm not only to rage around them, but to enter into them; the storm had become an internal experience; it had conquered. In Christ it remains outside Himself; it is conquered. In a passage of St John's Gospel, the Lord says that the Prince of the world has no power over Him. He is free, He has overcome the world; He can project on it the measure, the categories of eternity, stability, serenity, salvation, security, not the precarious and frail security of the little boat, but another security; not the peace, the naive peace of those who say 'That will never happen to me', or console others by saying 'Don't worry it won't happen to you', but the peace of one who has said 'It may happen, it will happen, it has happened, and yet because I have lost all human hope, I stand firm and unshaken on divine hope.'

I have said that Christ was at a certain point of the storm which we should reach in order to be with God in the storm; that Peter nearly drowned because he did not reach it. Where is this point? This point of the storm is not a point where there is no storm, it is what one calls the eye of the hurricane, it is the point where all conflicting forces meet and where an equipoise is reached not because there is no violence—not because there is no tension, not because there is no tragedy, but because the tragedy and the tension have come to such a pitch that they meet so forcibly as to balance each other; they are at the point of breaking. This is the point where God stands, and when we think of God, the God of history, the God of human life, the God Whom we accuse all the time, to Whom we give from time to time a chance by saying 'He must be right because He is God'—this is the God Who has chosen to stand at the breaking point of things, and this is why He can be respected, why we can treat Him with consideration, why we can believe in Him and not despise Him.

Now, where is this point? Long ago a man stood in

anguish, in despair, before the face of God and before the judgement of his friends. This man was called Job. He was afflicted with all that can afflict a man—bereavement, loss of all he possessed, loss of all that was dear, but more than this, more tragically than this, with the loss of understanding. He no longer could understand his God. Meaning had gone out of his life, and in his argument with God and in his argument with his friends, he stood for meaning and refused consolation; he refused to be consoled and extricated from tragedy and anguish by a comforting, appeasing and false image of God and His ways. He believed, indeed he knew, a living God, and that One he could no longer understand. And at a certain moment, he says, 'Where is the man that will stand between me and my Judge, who will put his hand on my shoulder and on my Judge's shoulder?' Where is he that will step into the situation, take a place at the heart of the conflict, at the breaking point of the tension, stand between the two in order to re-unite them, and to make them one? He had a sense that only that could be the solution of his problem; indeed of the problem of the meaning of tragedy, ultimately of the meaning of history. He had a presentiment that only that could be true, and that indeed happened. It happened when the Son of God became the Son of Man, when the Word of God became flesh, when Jesus came into the world, who being truly man, could put His hand on the man's shoulders without destroying the man by the fire of divine touch, and who could without blasphemy and sacrilege, put His hand on the shoulder of God without being destroyed.

This is what we truly mean by Intercession. This God is the one who stands at the middle of history. He is the one who stands at the breaking point of the storm, and He calls us to stand where He stands, to be involved, to be committed, to be committed to life and death within the storm, and yet neither to accept this fallacy of a ghost in the storm instead of God, or to turn to God and say 'If you can do nothing more, at least be together with us, in anguish and in despair.' He wants us to take a step, to be *in* the world at the point which I called 'the eye of the hurricane', but not *of* the world, because we are free from the uncertainty, from the fear, from the self-centredness of Peter, remembering himself at a moment when the whole sea was death and danger for the other disciples, for all the other boats around, and when God stood there as the key of harmony, but was not the harmony that he expected.

I should like to give you one example of what it means both to make an act of intercession and to stand in the place which is ours. It is the story of a woman of whom we know nothing except the name. She was called Natalie. The story was told me by the other people involved in it. In 1919 at a moment when the Civil War was raging like a storm over Russia, when our cities were falling prey to one army after the other, a woman with two young children was trapped in a city which had fallen into the hands of the Red Army, while her husband was an officer of the White Army. To save her life and theirs, she hid in a small cabin on the outskirts of the city. She wanted to wait until the first assaults were over and try to escape afterwards. On the second day someone knocked at her door towards the evening. She opened it in fear and she was confronted with a young woman of her own age. The woman said 'You must flee at once because you have been discovered and betrayed; you will be shot tonight.' The other woman, showing her children that stood there, said, 'How could we do that? We would be recognised at once, and they can't walk far.' The young woman who so far had been nothing but a neighbour, someone living next door, became that great thing which one calls a neighbour in the Gospel. She grew to the full stature of the Gospel of God, of the good news of the dignity and greatness of man, and she said 'They won't look for you, I shall stay behind.' And the mother said 'But they will kill you.' 'Yes,' said the woman, 'but I have no children, you must go.' And the mother went.

It is not easy, I would say it is almost sacrilegious, to try to imagine what happened in the heart and mind of this woman in the course of the hours that preceded her death. But we can look back to the Gospel and see what happened to those who were the prototype, the archetype of this great and holy woman.

Almost two thousand years before, a young man of her age was waiting for His death. His name was Jesus. He was in a garden wrapped in the darkness of the coming night. There was no reason within Him why He should die. He was young, healthy; He had done nothing wrong. He was waiting to die in a vicarious way other people's death. He was waiting in the darkness of the night, and death was coming to kill Life Eternal itself. Three times He went towards His disciples, hoping for a word that would strengthen His heart, for companionship, not to be released, not to be saved from the oncoming death, but to feel that there was a human presence, compassion, and love. The disciples were asleep. He got no help.

Natalie in the coming night, in the gathering darkness, in the cold that was falling from the walls and the roof, had nowhere to turn; there was no-one to whom she could turn. She was alone, facing the coming of another woman's death that would be enacted in her body, in her destiny. She could have walked out. The moment she had passed the threshold, she was again Natalie, not the

mother. Two thousand years before on that same cold
night when Christ was betrayed into the hands of His
murderers, the strongest, the most daring of His disciples
was challenged three times, twice by a little maid in the
courtyard, once by a group of bystanders. He was not
asked 'Are you Jesus?', he was told 'You were with him!'
and three times he said 'No', and walked out of the courtyard. Into what? Into security. He turned round and the
eyes of Christ met his eyes, and he remembered and he
wept. But he walked out. Natalie did not walk out, she
stayed inside.

How often must she have thought 'Is there any hope
that at least my sacrifice will be useful?' Again, two
thousand years ago a man, John the Baptist, was waiting
for death and before he died, when he knew that death
was inevitable, he sent two of his disciples to Christ to ask
Him 'Are you He for whom we waited, or shall we expect
another one?' That means 'If you are He, then my life of
asceticism, my loneliness, my preaching, my imprisonment and death, all the tragedy and hardship of my life,
make sense. But if you are not, then I have been betrayed
by God and by man, by my own inspiration and by the
Promise of the living God. Are you He,' Christ did not
give him a direct answer. He gave him the answer of the
prophet 'Go and tell him what you see—the blind see,
the lame walk and the poor proclaim the good news'—
news about God—news about man. The humility of the
one alongside the greatness of the other.

Natalie probably asked herself the same question—was
it in vain that she was dying? There was no answer, only
the hours passed, the cold of the early morning came and
with it, death. The door was brutally opened and they
did not even take the trouble of dragging her out. She was
shot where she was.

This is the answer which the Christian can give to the tragedy of history. The place where we must stand. Natalie stood where Christ had stood, and where indeed Christ stands now, risen in Heaven with His hands and sides seared with nails and the spear. He stands at the very heart of human history, human suffering, human death, human anguish and tragedy. But He stands there like a rock. He stands there firm, having endured everything, every human suffering in thought and body, and He says to us Christians, 'This is where *you* must stand, not in the dreamland of a faith that gives you the illusion that you are already in heaven while you have never been on earth. No, at the heart of human suffering and tragedy but with a faith unshaken, with the certainty that He who was expected by Job, has come.' And if we stand there, we may undergo all that was promised by Him. You remember the passage: 'Are you prepared and capable of drinking of the cup which I shall drink, of undergoing what I shall undergo?' 'Yes,' said His two disciples. This must be our answer, and when tragedy comes, we must answer again as Isaiah spoke: '"Whom shall I send?" said the Lord. "Here I am, Lord, send me."' Like a sheep among the wolves; like the Son of God among men.